THE QUILTER'S SON
Liam's Choice

WRITTEN BY
Samantha Jillian Bayarr

Also by Samantha Jillian Bayarr

Jacob's Daughter Amish Collection
Jacob's Daughter
Amish Winter Wonderland
Under the Mulberry Tree
Amish Winter of Promises
Chasing Fireflies
Amish Summer of Courage
Under the Harvest Moon

Amish Romance
The Quilter's Son
An Amish Christmas Wish

Amish Love Series
An Amish Harvest
An Amish Courtship
An Amish Widower
Amish Sisters

LWF Amish Series
Little Wild Flower Book I
Little Wild Flower Book II
The Taming of a Wild Flower
Little Wild Flower in Bloom
Little Wild Flower's Journey

Christian Romance
Milk Maid in Heaven
The Anniversary

Christian Historical Romance
A Sheriff's Legacy: Book One
Preacher Outlaw: Book Two
Cattle Rustler in Petticoats: Book Three

**Please note: All editions may not be available yet.
Please check online for availability.**

Chapter 1

Goshen, Indiana

"Why did you hit me?" Liam worked his jaw back and forth, the sting of the slap causing his ear to ring. But more than that, she'd crushed his spirit with one blow.

Lucy doubled her fists and planted them on her hips. She knew she would later need to take a knee and beg forgiveness, but for now, she was content with her outburst. "Did it knock any sense into you? I can give it another try if it will change your mind."

Furry showed in Lucy's eyes, her face twisted in anger. But there was something else that showed in her eyes. Fear lay just below the surface where she tried very hard to hide it.

Liam felt caught between elation that she cared so much, grief over knowing how much he would miss her when he was gone, and irritation that she would defy the commitment of peace among the Amish.

"I'm not changing my mind. You can hit me a hundred times and it won't make me stay here. I want to be on my own and explore the world. Ever since my *daed* died last month, it's made me wonder if there was more to life than what we see in our secluded little corner of this community. I feel stifled here. Computers and cell phones interest me. And I've always wanted to learn how to build more than barns. I want to design houses, and to do that, I have to learn from outside construction companies. The only opportunity I have here is plowing the same fields my *daed* did his entire life. I want more out of life than that, and my *daed* knew that. When I die, I want my life to mean something."

Lucy looked at him through the veil of tears that blurred her vision. "You really think your *daed's* life amounted to nothing?"

"*Mei daed* knew I didn't want to be a farmer. That's why he let me go to the public school behind my *mamm's* back. With only three weeks left of my senior year after he died, I continued to go so I could graduate because I'm more determined than ever to get out of this backward society."

Lucy's lips formed a grim line, and tears spilled from her eyes. "If you think being Amish is *backward,* then perhaps you're correct in saying you don't belong here. But at least have the decency to face your *mamm* instead of sneaking out the window ·this late at night."

Liam kicked at the knapsack that rested against the large oak tree that stood beside the *haus*. It was almost too dark to see the expression on Lucy's face, but what he saw of it, he didn't like. "You didn't complain any of those nights I snuck out the window to meet with you."

"That's because I thought you had intended to marry me. Now I find out you stole that first kiss from me that I was saving for my husband; I can never get that back."

Liam braced his hands on her forearms. "Then come with me. We can still get married. We can get a little apartment and live in the city."

Lucy broke from his grasp, her face curling with disgust. "I could never get married without my *familye*. And I won't marry a *mann* who isn't baptized."

Liam picked up his knapsack and flung the weight of it over one shoulder. "Then I suppose we will be parting ways. If I take the baptism I will be destined to be just like my *daed*."

Lucy sobbed. "Would that really be so bad? How do you think he would feel if he could see you now running away from your *familye* like a coward?"

Liam yanked the straw hat from his head and tossed it to the ground. "He isn't here. My *mamm* and *schweschder* will be better off without me. As long as I don't want to be here, my heart isn't in it. So what's the point in staying? So I can make them as miserable as I am? Besides, Lydia no longer talks to me, and *mamm* doesn't talk to either of us. All she does is sit at her quilting frame and sew quilts. Neither of them will even notice I'm gone."

Lucy sniffled, closing the space between them. "Even if they don't, I will."

Liam backed away from her. If he kissed her now, he would never have the courage to leave. He didn't want things to end between them; he loved her a great deal, but he guessed it wasn't enough to make him want to stay. If he changed his mind it wouldn't be because of the opinion or request of another person. He had to stay for himself, and that wasn't how he felt. His desire to go was too strong to let anything or anyone get in his way—even if that meant he would have to break the heart of the woman he loved.

Lucy found it difficult to breathe. How could Liam do this to his *familye*—to her? Suddenly all the excuses he'd given her over the past few years regarding his busyness had made sense. He was too busy because he'd been leading a double life. Going to school all day and then working his chores around such a demanding schedule. Was he leaving her because he didn't think she was smart enough for him? Did he want someone better than her?

"Will you at least give it some more thought? Have you even prayed about it?"

Liam looked away. He hadn't prayed about it in the past month. He hadn't reached out to *Gott* about much since his *daed* died. He didn't want to hear the answer his heart was nudging him toward. He'd had his mind made up for some time, and now that he was eighteen, it was time.

Lucy nodded. "Your silence tells me you haven't prayed. Since you are so determined to abandon your *familye* and your faith, will you at least tell me where you're going so I can visit you?"

Liam paused. "*Nee,* it will be too far. I'm heading toward Michigan."

He didn't tell her that he was too nervous to go too far. Most likely, he would stay in Indiana and go to South Bend where his friends planned on renting a small house. He feared that if Lucy knew he would be living only a few miles away, she would constantly nag him about returning home.

Lucy lifted her chin in defiance. "If you're determined to go, then don't come back because I won't be waiting for you."

Her statement hurt worse than the slap she'd delivered across his face just a few moments earlier. Liam watched his future walk away from him, as he told himself a better future waited for him in the next town over. They'd both made their decision, and now they would have to live with it. Liam was confident he had his *daed's* blessing to leave, and that was all that mattered at the moment.

Chapter 2

South Bend, Indiana

"I still look Amish," Liam complained as he studied his appearance in the dressing room mirror.

"I'm going to need a haircut."

He had chosen the clothing store in the mall, after his new roommate, Steve, advised him that the store carried the latest styles. He liked the casual look of the sweatshirt and jeans, but his hair still gave him away. A quick stop at the barber shop would get rid of all traces of the Amish in him. But it couldn't erase the pull he still felt in his heart. At eighteen, his biggest desire was to stay as far away from the Amish community as possible, and leave the pain of losing his *daed* behind him once and for all.

His *mamm* had no idea he'd been sneaking away to the public school for the past four years to get his diploma. His *daed* had helped him hide it from his *mamm,* but after the accident, his *mamm* was too consumed with grief to even notice Liam's antics when he continued to go. His twin sister, Lydia, was too busy caring for the house and doing all the things their *mamm* used to do before the buggy accident that took their father's life, so she hadn't noticed either.

It was a tough time for everyone, and Liam was responsible for the upkeep of the farm. Spending all day in school and keeping up with his studies was difficult to do with a farm to maintain, but he'd been determined to leave home and start a new life for himself, leaving Lydia to take over in his absence.

He was now finished with his senior year and needed the diploma to get a job out in the *real world,* as he'd come to know it. His friends at school had guided him every step of the way, right down to teaching him how to drive a car and how to dress and act so he could hide his heritage from the outside world. The transition had not been an easy one, but it was what he felt he needed to do to stifle the grief he still held onto over his father's death.

Liam's refusal of the Bishop's prompting to receive the baptism to seal his Amish roots had not gone over well with anyone. He felt guilty for leaving his *mamm* and *schweschder,* but he didn't see his leaving would change things much. He'd been a coward and left his *mamm* a note letting her know he was leaving, but he didn't think about how it would affect her. His being there had gone unnoticed when his family stopped functioning after his *daed's* accident.

Liam determinedly put the memories behind him, unable to imagine the regret that would hound him over the next few years…

Chapter 3

Seven years later...

A summer breeze rustled the leaves on the trees in front of the shops that lined Main Street in Goshen. Being a typical July morning in Indiana, steamy mist rose from the dew-drenched patches of grass that lined the walkways as the sun warmed up the earth. Liam stood across the street behind a maple tree, hoping his mother and his sister would not notice him watching them. He knew the nature of the Amish was to walk with downcast eyes when in public because he'd spent the first eighteen years of his life doing the same, but he feared his mother would somehow sense his presence and look his way. Since he'd left home, he'd grown into a man—an *Englischer*. But that wouldn't stop a mother from recognizing her own son, would it?

When his mother and sister entered the small quilt shop, he noticed his mother had used a key to open the door. He knew the insurance company of the driver of the car that had killed his father had presented his mother with a sizable settlement, and he wondered now if she'd finally used it to open the shop. Part of him wanted to go to her and ease the worry lines that creased her aging face, but too much time had passed. A reunion would only open old wounds. Since he hadn't taken the baptism, his actions had not earned him a shunning, but that wouldn't keep his family from turning a cold shoulder to him—something he felt he deserved.

Even if he were to approach them, he knew he couldn't handle the pain of rejection from his own mother and sister. Shame crept into his heart for his act of betrayal toward his family and the community. He felt like a coward, and he had to admit that his life away from them had been empty and lonely. He'd thrown himself into his work, earning enough money working for others to start his own business. Now with seven men that counted on him, he felt the strain even more.

They'd only had a few big jobs so far this year, and if he didn't bring in more work soon, his company would perish, along with all his hard work. But what had it all been for? To escape a community shunned by the outside world, only to trade it for being shunned by the people he loved most? Now, as he stood across the street watching his mother and sister enter *The Quilter's Square,* Liam suddenly questioned the decision he'd made seven long years ago…

ജ്ഞ

Nellie Yoder felt a breeze brush by her, and with it came the feeling she was being watched. Out of the corner of her eye, she spotted the *Englischer* again; he was standing across the street as if waiting for an invitation from her. She felt his presence, the same as if she were still carrying him in her womb. After all, a mother knows her own flesh and blood. She had managed to swallow the lump that formed in her throat and compose herself for the sake of the *dochder* who had not left her side during the years since her husband's death. Nellie longed to hold her son and tell him how much he'd been missed, but only time would tell if such a dream could become reality.

She ushered Lydia into the quilt shop before the girl noticed her twin brother loitering across the street. What had she been thinking when she'd opened this shop? She knew that it needed repairs that she couldn't fix on her own. She'd known about Liam's business for several months, and thought it would give her the opportunity to bring her son home where he belonged. Her plan was to hire him to do the renovations, hoping it would draw him back to his *familye* and the community.

Now, as she saw him for the third day in a row, Nellie suddenly wondered if she should have thought things through a little more clearly. After all these years of letting her husband's settlement sit idle, she wondered if using it to get her son back was the wisest thing she could have done. She feared that because so much time had passed, he would be more resistant to returning to the community. But after seeing him watching her again this morning, she was convinced she'd made the right move. She knew she would have to proceed with caution, so as not to upset Lydia or spook Liam. She didn't want him to run from her, but so far, he'd not approached her either. She sighed deeply as she watched him walk away, knowing it was too late to abandon her plan now. The first step had already been taken.

Chapter 4

Lydia tried not to alert her *mamm*, who hadn't seemed to notice her own son standing across the street watching them for the third day this week. The urge to talk to her estranged twin outweighed any fear of getting her heart broken again if he should turn his back on them all over again. Her heart ached to run to him and talk to him like they hadn't since they were mere children on the farm—before the tragedy that tore their *familye* apart, and before Liam left them to fend for themselves.

Lydia felt a mixture of anger and love for her *bruder*, if that was possible. She knew that approaching him would put her and her *mamm* at risk of being reprimanded by the Bishop, but she wasn't sure she cared at this point. Too much time had been lost, and too much suffering had consumed their *familye* already.

Guilt crept back into her heart as she momentarily replayed the day her *bruder* left them.

For years, she'd wondered if her harsh words had pushed Liam further into his decision to leave. She'd discovered he'd been attending the public school, and had scolded him for thinking only of himself. That day he'd asked her to attend his high school graduation, and she'd refused. She'd accused him of being selfish and had told him to leave. She hadn't meant it, and she'd regretted those words ever since that day.

Even now, no matter how much her love for her *bruder* tugged at Lydia's heart, logic reminded her how difficult life would be for her *mamm* if she were to get her hopes up regarding her son's return to the community—especially if he rejected them again. Lydia had been the one who'd stayed, but she hadn't taken the baptism. She'd remained with their *mamm* all these years and shouldered the responsibility on her own.

For weeks after Liam ran off, Lydia had waited for him to return, hoping that he would get a taste of the outside world but that it would be so difficult he would return home. When weeks turned to months, and months turned to years, hope for such a miracle had nearly dwindled to nothing—until three days ago.

ജരൂ

Lucy Graber watched out the bay window of her bakery front as she stacked cookies and pastries in the display case under the counter that ran the length of the store. For three days now, she'd watched the handsome stranger linger across the street in the early morning hours.

There was a familiarity about him that she couldn't quite push aside. She had all but convinced herself that the *Englischer* was Liam Yoder, but she didn't dare hope for such a foolish thing. She had given up hope of his return too many years ago to count. Before his *daed* died, the two of them had been seeing one another secretly, and even though their love was still fairly new, Lucy had been convinced she would marry him one day. Within days after the tragedy struck his *familye*, Liam began to pull away from Lucy. They'd shared their first and last kiss in the early morning hours before the accident that had taken the life of Liam's *daed*. Lucy had felt Liam's promise in that kiss—a promise that would never come to pass.

೫೮೧೩

Liam hung his head as he walked down the street toward his work truck. He hadn't realized just how much his heart ached from the separation from his family until seeing them again. But he felt too much shame to approach them. He was supposed to go into town with his father the morning of the accident. Instead, he'd been out too late with Lucy, and had fallen asleep in the barn after chores. He vaguely remembered his dad finding him in the hayloft and telling him to stay put, that he would run the errands in town alone. He'd never been able to shake the guilt of allowing his dad to go without him. Guilt had overcome Liam knowing that if only he'd been with his father, he could have done something to save his life that morning. His lack of responsibility that day had destroyed his family and cost him a future with Lucy.

When his cell phone rang, Liam pulled it from his back pocket and held it to his ear.

"Hey boss," Steve said. "You on your way in? We got a call for a new job this morning. We're expected on the site in two hours to give an estimate. Sounds like a big one."

The news of a job lifted Liam's spirits. "I'm on my way."

He hung up the phone and looked back toward the quilting shop one last time before hopping into his truck and driving away.

Chapter 5

Liam's heart did a flip-flop against his chest wall when Steve showed him the name of the shop owner that was requesting an estimate. How could he go to his mother's shop and mingle with his family when they probably didn't have any desire to talk to him since he'd forsaken them? There were two Yoder's Construction companies in the area; why had his mother chosen his? Was it the name she trusted, or had she known it was his company when she'd made the call? The other Yoder Construction was closer to them as it was in Goshen, but the majority of their work was building houses from start to finish, while Liam and his crew did mostly repair and reconstructive work out of South Bend. He'd always hoped he could build houses, but things just hadn't turned out that way.

"Why don't you take this one, Steve? I have a possible job on the other side of town to check on. It's another small one, but at least it's honest work."

Liam was suddenly grateful that he'd taken the call about the other job on the way back to his office. Though he had first intended on sending Steve to get the estimate for the smaller job across town, his only focus now was delaying an awkward reunion with his family. Getting the estimate for his mother had changed everything.

"Are you sure, Boss? This is a pretty big job and I don't want to give the wrong figures."

Liam patted his friend on the back. "You have to learn sometime, Steve. Besides, I trust you to bring all the particulars back to the office so we can go over it before giving the shop owner a final estimate."

Liam wasn't sure how he would handle the job if they took it, but he also couldn't leave his family to work with another contractor that might not do the job as well as he would. He cringed at the thought of someone taking advantage of his mother and charging her too much for less than perfect work. His own skills were by no means perfected, but he knew his mother and what would make her happy—at least he used to.

ဆာ

Liam paced the length of his office until he heard Steve's truck pull into the parking lot. What had taken the man so long to get the estimate from his mother? Had she told Steve she was his *mamm?* Steve had known he'd grown up Amish, but Liam had never told any of the guys he worked with about his past. It had never come up, and Liam never felt comfortable sharing anything so private with any of them. As far as they knew, he was their boss, and that was good enough for them. Aside from a few of the guys sharing that their wives nagged them to come home early all the time, none of them ever openly shared anything too personal about their lives, and that was how Liam preferred it.

Steve entered the office and put his clipboard down on Liam's desk with a huff.

"Whoever sold that woman the property ought to be ashamed of himself. The plumbing and electrical all needs to be updated and up to code. The ceiling has holes and rotted tiles from a leak somewhere. And the walls are rotted and crumbling. The place looks like there was a fire."

If memory served him, Liam recalled a fire that had consumed several of the shops in the downtown district a couple of years back, but nearly all of them had been renovated since then. The outside sign looked outdated—probably belonging to the previous owner. But if he knew his *mamm* as much he thought he did, she would have taken it literally as a sign she was meant to have the shop—no matter what condition it was in. Had she planned to hire him from the time she'd signed the papers of ownership on the place? His mother was too smart to be sold a dilapidated property—unless she had other plans for it. Plans that involved him.

⍏⍎

Nellie was a little more than disappointed that her own son had sent one of his employees to take the assessment of her repairs. The *mann* had told her he would need to take them back to the office to consult with his boss before giving a full estimate. She'd hoped to finally see her son face-to-face, but it seemed *Gott* had other plans for her today.

After being pointed out all the faults the shop held, she was confident it would be enough to keep Liam and his crew around long enough for her to repair her relationship with him while he repaired her shop. She prayed he wasn't avoiding her by not coming to give the estimate, but perhaps it was not something he did on a regular basis. After all, her son was the boss—of his own company. Nellie couldn't be more proud, unless he chose to return to the Amish ways. But that was a prayer for another day.

⊷∝⊷

Lydia watched her *mamm's* face fall when the young *mann* walked into the shop wearing a blue shirt with the name *Yoder Construction* embroidered on the pocket. She wondered if her *mamm* knew it was Liam's company, and she'd hoped he would show up. Unsure of her *mamm's* source of disappointment, she didn't dare bring up her *bruder* in case her *mamm* didn't know about him just yet. She would soon enough, and they would deal with it then—together—as a *familye*.

ะ€Cะ

Lucy balanced the plate of cookies in one hand and a pitcher of iced tea in the other, three paper cups tucked under her arm as she entered Nellie's quilt shop.

Nellie looked up as the door squeaked open and her neighbor entered.

Lucy smiled. "I thought you might want some refreshment. It's such a warm day today."

Nellie approached the young girl and took the tea and cups from her, setting them down on a table she'd brought from the farm. "*Danki*. This place is going to need more work than I originally thought. It seems it needs more than just a thorough cleaning."

Lucy looked around. "I was lucky *mei daed* had my shop cleaned and fixed before he gave it to me for my eighteenth birthday. I think he decided I might as well have something to fall back on since it wasn't likely I'd be taking a husband. He was right because here I am seven years later, and still without a husband."

Nellie felt sorry for Lucy. She knew that she was sweet on her only son, and it broke her heart that the two of them weren't giving her any *grandkinner*.

"Don't give up hope, dear Lucy. You never know what *Gott* has waiting for you just around the corner. You're still young. You shouldn't give up hope. He could bless you when least you expect it."

Lucy hoped the woman was right. Was it too late to hope that Liam would come back to her?

Chapter 6

"But Boss," Steve protested. "Don't you think you should let Henry go do the smaller job so you can come with me and rest of the guys to the big job? I know you're the boss, but this will be our *biggest* job this year."

Liam shook his head. "I can finish painting the house in three days, tops. Those first few days at the quilt shop will be spent assessing, measuring, and making a list of all the supplies needed. By the time I finish at the other place, you'll be ready to start this one. I have faith in you. Besides, Henry has more experience than I do with this stuff. But I'll expect a full report at the end of each day."

Steve tipped his cap toward Liam. "You're the boss."

Liam managed a half-smile. "That's what they tell me."

He knew he would eventually have to show up at his mother's quilt shop to do the job she'd hired his company to do, but a few days would give him enough time to prepare for their first meeting after so many years apart. It wouldn't be easy seeing her again, and Liam hoped she wouldn't fire him and his men when she discovered who it was she'd actually hired.

Liam grabbed a cup of coffee for the road and headed toward the paint job, while his crew went the opposite direction to his mother's quilt shop. His heart ached to see his family again, but he just wasn't ready yet. He hadn't realized just how much he'd missed them until he'd seen them quite by accident that first day outside of the quilt shop.

Liam had actually been on his way into the bakery next door to the quilt shop that first morning when he'd happened upon his mother and sister. After hearing from Steve about a pastry he'd purchased at the bakery that tasted like Christmas, he knew he had to check it out. He'd only known of one person in his life that could make the sort of pastry his employee had described, and he'd had to see for himself if what he suspected was true. When he happened upon his mother and sister that morning instead, thoughts of Lucy Graber and her pastries had left his mind—until now.

Liam couldn't be sure what it was that triggered the memory of Lucy, but perhaps it was the roses that bordered the porch of the house he was about to paint. He used to pick roses from his mother's garden and bring them to Lucy when they would steal away late after dark to spend a few moments together when they were young. She'd always allowed the sweetest little giggle to escape her lips whenever he would bring her roses. Then her cheeks would flame from the embarrassment. Liam had thought she was the prettiest girl he'd ever seen. But Lucy was surely married by now with several *kinner;* he was certain of it. There was no sense in going to the bakery only to be disappointed when he wasn't certain he would find her there. But if he'd known she was possibly working just a few miles from where he'd been living, he'd have gone to see her long before this.

Liam's biggest problem now was how to handle the meeting with his mother and sister while his employees stood by and watched. He hadn't told any of them of his past, with the exception of Steve, who'd gone to school with him. But the two of them had buried that secret a long time ago. He hoped his employees wouldn't think any differently of him if they were to find out his secret. After all, everyone has a past. If any of them would be accepting, Henry would be the most understanding. After spending several years in jail for stealing building supplies from his former employer, he was grateful for Liam's ability to overlook his past. Given the older man's past history, he was lucky to have a job, and he was very much aware of that fact. Liam had been the only construction company to give the man a chance, and he was glad he had. Not only was Henry a hard worker, he taught Liam things that improved his skills as a contractor.

Wiping the sweat from his brow, Liam considered holding a meeting with his staff as he prepped the house for painting. He'd spent the past hour scraping chips of old paint from the backside of the house, and now he was ready to begin painting. The wood siding was weather-worn, but luckily, the back was the only side that had begun to chip and peel.

If I held a meeting, what would I say to them? Maybe it would be better if I just wing it. If they're caught off guard, they may let it go and not say anything in front of my familye. But there's always the chance either my mamm or my schweschder will not even speak to me.

Chapter 7

Nellie continued to scrub the floors of her new quilt shop while the *menner* from her son's company took measurements and wrote things on clipboards. So far her plan to spend time with Liam had backfired on her. She was more than disappointed when he didn't show up with the others, but her ears perked up when she overheard one of the *menner* say that Liam was at another job for the next few days. By the end of the week, she would be reunited with her son.

In some ways, she was grateful for the extra time, hoping that when he did show up he wouldn't take his *menner* and leave since they'd already begun the job for her. Nellie felt the timing was to her advantage, and so she determined to be patient for her long-awaited meeting with her only son. She wondered how her *dochder* would react when she finally came face-to-face with the twin *bruder* she felt had betrayed his *familye*. Nellie was ready to forgive him for acting like a foolish child and welcome him back into their lives. But would Lydia feel the same way?

"Lydia, would you mind helping me bring in the boxes from the buggy?"

Lydia was happy to get some fresh air. All the dust being stirred up from the workers was making her cough. With the exception of one of the *menner* called *Steve,* Lydia wasn't interested in being around any of them. She'd caught Steve glancing in her direction more than once, and she hoped her *mamm* hadn't noticed. Normally Lydia would never even consider flirting with an *Englischer*, but he had started it, and she wasn't opposed to the idea. Her cousin, Miriam, had dated an *Englischer,* and it had worked out wonderfully for the two of them. Jonathon had taken the baptismal classes and received the baptism, and in the end, Miriam and Jonathon had been married by the Bishop, and are now expecting their first *boppli*.

Lydia shied away from Steve's frequent glances, fearful that he would be able to pick up on her intimate thoughts. If her *mamm* knew she'd been thinking such things, she would be scolded for sure and for certain.

With her own *bruder* as an *Englischer,* Lydia wasn't exactly sure where her thoughts stood on the matter. But the idea of dating an *Englischer* seemed a little more rebellious than she was willing to be for the time-being. Since she hadn't taken the baptism, she wouldn't be shunned for such an action. Lydia wasn't altogether satisfied with her decision not to take the baptism, but it had made sense at the time her *bruder* had left. Truth be told, there were times when she'd second-guessed her lack of commitment to the community, but she wanted to keep her options open as long as was possible. Did her *bruder* know something she didn't? Had being an *Englischer* made him happy? He seemed to be doing alright for himself, but there would be no real way of knowing the truth unless she spoke to him. But the first question that she would have for Liam would be to ask why he hadn't looked back after he'd left.

Chapter 8

Lucy couldn't help but stare out of the bakery window when several *menner* showed up at Nellie's quilting shop next door. They all wore the same blue shirts with the same logo on the pocket that she'd seen the handsome blond stranger wearing. She hadn't seen him loitering across the street yet this morning, and wondered if he would show up. She'd known Liam was interested in construction when he'd left the community, but was it really possible the handsome stranger was him? They'd had a heated discussion about his desire to have his own company just before he'd left. She'd begged him to stay, but he was determined to stand on his own—away from the community.

Lucy looked for the handsome *mann* she thought to be *her* Liam, but he was not with the others when they'd arrived. Part of her wished he would come around again so she could settle the dispute in her mind once and for all, but her heart dreaded the possibility of being broken all over again. Most days, she was able to keep thoughts of Liam out of her mind, but every so often, a memory of him would find its way into her thoughts. Since she'd seen the handsome stranger hanging out across the street from the bakery the past few days, her mind had become consumed with thoughts of Liam again.

A loud crash interrupted her thoughts. How long had she been standing at the window staring out at nothing? The noise had come from the quilt shop next door. With no customers in the bakery, Lucy decided to rush over there to see if everyone was alright.

෫ඏൠ

Liam wiped the paint from his hands before answering his cell phone. It was the third time it had rung, and he knew that meant it was one of his men. He hadn't wanted to answer it because he feared they would ask him to stop by the quilt shop, and he wasn't ready for that just yet.

Holding the phone to his ear with two fingers, Liam anticipated the request from the other end.

"Boss, we need you over here right away. Part of the ceiling collapsed."

Liam's heart lurched forward against his ribcage. "Was anyone hurt?"

Steve coughed. "The owner and her daughter were outside when it happened. I was the only one inside, but I was in the back near the circuit breaker at the time. How soon can you be here?"

Liam looked at the half-painted home he'd been working on most of the day. "If no one was hurt, rope off the area and ask the owner to stay clear until you can be sure there won't be more damage. I'm in the middle of painting, and it would take me at least an hour of cleanup and travel to get there. You can handle this without me. Give my apologies to the owner and explain that I'm in the middle of a job I can't leave right now. I'll be sure to go over with you first thing tomorrow morning."

Steve agreed, but Liam could tell he wasn't buying the excuse he was trying to convince him of. Liam couldn't prevent the ceiling from caving in any more than his employees could. But it was his responsibility to ensure the safety of this crew *and* his family. Guilt consumed him as he continued to paint the small house. He knew he would have to give the paint job to one of the other guys so he could see to the safety of his mother's quilt shop.

ಬಾಂಗ್

Lucy overheard one of the workers calling his boss, which she assumed was Liam. From the worker's end of the conversation, she concluded that the boss had no intention of seeing to the crisis that had unfolded at the quilt shop. Had Liam's exposure to the outside world compromised his integrity? The Liam she had grown to love in her teen years would never have turned his back on his family. But he did, in fact, do that very thing when he became old enough to do so. Was he still so bitter even now that his *familye* still meant nothing to him?

Lucy comforted Nellie, who seemed distraught at the company owner's refusal to see the importance of the immediate danger that the collapsed ceiling posed.

"He doesn't seem like a respectable business owner," Lucy offered.

Nellie held up a hand in defense. "*Nee,* we can't judge a *mann* simply because he isn't able to be here. That Steve fellow said he was stuck at another job and would be here in the morning to check on things. Mr. Yoder recommended we stay out of the building until then, and I think that's wise."

Lucy felt a little unnerved at Nellie's reaction to the recommendation from the company owner they hadn't even met. Was she aware that her son could possibly be the owner? Was Lucy sure of what she'd seen? Perhaps it was best if she herself did not jump to conclusions in order to avoid any possible misunderstanding. Still, she was more than curious to know what his reasons were for not taking this job more seriously, whether he was Liam or not. One thing was certain in Lucy's mind; if the owner of the company Nellie hired was indeed Liam, she now saw him as a bigger coward than she had when they were teenagers.

Nellie and Lydia packed the boxes back into the buggy, intending to leave for the day. Nellie couldn't help but feel discouraged regarding the delay she would endure in opening her shop. More than that, she was disappointed in her only son. Had he become a coward?

Chapter 9

Liam felt confident leaving the paint job in the capable hands of his youngest employee. The young man was the best one who could operate the expensive paint sprayer he'd invested in, so Liam let the job go and followed the others in his white 4x4 to his mother's quilt shop.

Had his men seen how nervous he was before they'd left the office? He had prayed the entire morning, and even breathed a few prayers now while he kept his eye on the road. There was a lot riding on this meeting; it could decide his fate in more ways than one. If all else failed, he would be professional and business-like in order to keep the job for the sake of the men who counted on him so they could pay their bills this month. He would do whatever he could to protect this job from falling through. His personal vested interest in the job and his family would have to be put aside.

When he parked his truck in the alley behind the shops on Main Street, Liam paused and took a deep breath before getting out, asking God for grace. He knew he had a lot of years to make up for to his mother and sister, and it wouldn't be easy even if they allowed him to.

Lord, soften the hearts of my family, and pave the way for me to reunite with them. Bless me with the courage to face them and to endure the heartache if they should choose not to forgive me for abandoning them.

When Liam noticed his crew gathered around his truck, he knew he'd stalled long enough. One more deep breath and Liam swung open his door, easing himself out of his truck. It was now or never, and *never* was just not an option at this point. He tried to swallow the bile that threatened to enter his throat. He would be strong and accept whatever reaction his mother and sister had. He didn't regret being out on his own and starting a business, but he knew he couldn't keep his business and his family too. It had to be one or the other. He had no intention of returning to the community, and that would be the hardest part to make his mother understand.

Liam allowed the others to go ahead of him, while he hung back and examined the damage from the door. His family did not seem to be in the building, so he quickly busied himself checking for major structural damage. His chest tightened when he heard the front door swing open. His back was to the door, and he couldn't bring himself to turn around.

Liam felt his mother's eyes bore into the back of his head. He could hear that she hadn't moved from the entryway, as if his presence had flash-frozen her in place.

ঙ০ଓ

Lucy stifled every impulse in her to keep from marching over to the quilting shop and demanding to know if the handsome stranger was indeed Liam Yoder. When he stepped out of the white pickup truck, she could see in the blue of his eyes how much he resembled her old beau. When he'd left the Amish community, he'd taken her future hope of marrying and having *kinner* with him.

It's been seven years. Why am I still so chafed about his leaving? I've had plenty of offers since then. Maybe I should have accepted one of them. Except none of them made me happy the way Liam had.

Lucy sighed as she watched her last customer leave the shop. She knew there would be a gap between this one and her lunch rush, but she intended to keep busy, hoping it would take her mind off of what was going on next door. Part of her didn't have the heart to interrupt what she hoped would be a pleasant reunion between Liam and his *familye*. But the part of her that still held onto a little bit of anger for him wanted to storm over there and demand an explanation. Deep down, she knew she didn't have the courage to confront him. Despite her outburst the last time she'd seen Liam, Lucy had been brought up to remain silent rather than voice unpleasant words toward another, but that didn't stop her from feeling the strong desire to do just that.

Nellie stopped in her tracks when she entered her quilt shop. Her own son stood only a few feet from her—the son she hadn't seen in seven years. Her *dochder,* Lydia, who stood next to her, reached out for her hand. Neither of them moved except to cling to one another. Nellie's mouth went dry, preventing her from finding her voice. She watched Liam move further into the depth of the shop as Steve approached them.

"Good to see you again, Mrs. Yoder," Steve said, then tipped his ball-cap toward Lydia. "Miss Yoder."

Lydia's heart beat a little faster as she made eye contact with Steve.

He pointed toward the back of the long shop. "That's my boss, Liam Yoder." Looking between the two, he did a double-take. "I hadn't realized until now that he has the same last name as you do."

Nellie wasn't sure what to say, so she nodded. She figured it was best not to say anything until she'd had the chance to speak to her son away from his employees. It was obvious that he hadn't told them she was his *mamm,* but Liam was a mirror image of his *daed* and looked nothing like her or Lydia. Pain pricked Nellie's heart at the thought of her own son rejecting her like that. He'd left a lot of hurt in his wake when he'd left home so long ago, but Nellie had tried to fill the void by telling herself it was only temporary. But when weeks turned to months and months turned to years, she'd given up hope of ever setting eyes on him again. Now, here he was, only a few feet from her, and she couldn't muster up the courage to pull Liam into her arms and tell him she'd missed him. Although she had to admit, part of her wanted to take him into the barn and give him a sound lashing for his behavior.

Chapter 10

Liam's heart sped up at the mention of his name. He turned, not looking his mother or sister in the eye. He nodded politely. "Ma'am."

Nellie's throat constricted at the sound of his voice. She noticed immediately that he'd spoken to her using ma'am out of respect rather than using *mamm* as a term of endearment. This was not going to be easy.

Liam began to explain how he intended to put her shop back together to make it good as new, but Nellie didn't hear a word he said. She was too busy biting her bottom lip to keep from sobbing and pulling her son into her arms. He'd grown to be a handsome *mann*—an *Englischer*. If he didn't look so much like his *daed,* she would think he'd managed to fool everyone—everyone but her. Did he think he could come in here and convince her of his act of not knowing her? She could see the fear in his eyes. He knew. He knew that he couldn't hide that from his own *mamm*. Didn't he?

Liam could hear his voice cracking as though he were another person listening to his voice. He wasn't even sure of what he was saying to his mother. All he could think about was how much he'd missed her. But he'd be lucky to keep the job now that she knew it was *his* company that she'd hired to do the renovations to her quilt shop. He hoped she wouldn't fire him and his men. They needed the work, and he intended to do right by his mother for the first time since his dad had died.

He looked into his mother's eyes trying to read her mood. Had she forgiven him for betraying her, or was she being polite the way he was? She seemed pleasant but worried. The lines on her face had deepened since the last time he'd seen her. Her dark brown hair was peppered with gray, and the dark circles surrounding her eyes implied how much sleep she'd probably lost over the past seven years.

Her cordial tone made him nervous. When he was a young boy, the woman could unravel any mischief he'd been up to with only her tone of voice and the look she was giving him now.

I'm a grown man now. I can handle this.

"We expect the renovations to take about three weeks, but as soon as we get the mess cleared away from the ceiling collapse, you should be able to get back in here and work around us. Can you give us until the end of the week to get this mess cleaned up so it's safe for you and your daughter?"

He could see his mother cringe at the formal comment he'd made.

She tipped her mouth into a smile. "Of course, Mr. Yoder, but my *dochder* and I would rather stay and help clean things up."

Liam could see his mother had no intention of budging on the matter. "That's fine as long as you steer clear from the back of the store where the damage is the worst. I can't guarantee your safety back there."

Nellie nodded.

Steve and Jonny flashed Liam a strange look.

"Hey Boss, can we talk to you for a minute outside?"

Liam tipped his hat to his mother and sister before following his employees into the alley.

"What gives?" Jonny complained. "You know we can't have those women in the store when we're trying to clean this mess up. What if they get hurt? We'll all have to give up our pay to take care of their hospital bills."

"I don't think Amish people go to hospitals," Steve said, directing his comment toward Liam.

"Yeah, they are kind of backward, aren't they?" Jonny said with a chuckle.

Even though Liam had said the same thing several times, hearing it from someone else grated on his nerves.

"The daughter is kinda pretty. I'd go out with her," Jonny added.

Liam's breath caught in his throat, causing him to choke. He clenched his fists as he coughed to clear his throat. He wanted to yell at Jonny *That's my sister you're talking about,* but Lydia hadn't been his sister for the past seven years. Still, it was *his* duty to protect her, and he would not let the likes of Jonny lay a hand on Lydia. But as he thought about it, she wouldn't find a better Christian man for her than Steve, who stood politely at his side. The two of them had been friends since high school; Steve had even stood by him during his struggle with his dad's death.

"Let's keep our minds on the current issue," Liam ordered. "The Amish are hard workers, and I'm sure she feels the need to help because it's her shop."

"Since when do you know so much about Amish folks?" Jonny asked.

Liam ignored his flippant remark and turned to address Steve who knew of his past.

"Let the women remain, but everyone is responsible for keeping an eye on them."

Jonny pulled off his ball cap and slapped it against his leg in frustration. "Okay, but if they get hurt, I'm not giving up my pay to send them to the hospital."

Steve waited until Jonny stormed off, and then turned to Liam. "Don't tell me that's your family. I'd almost forgotten you were Amish."

Liam swallowed the lump in his throat. "That is my mother and my sister. I am freaking out a little and don't know how to deal with them. Seeing them again makes me realize how much I've missed them."

Steve clapped him on the shoulder. "Then tell them that. It's a good place to start, isn't it?"

Liam crossed over to his mother's buggy and petted the familiar horse. "It isn't that easy, Steve. The Amish are closed off from the rest of the world. I haven't been shunned, but her strong bond to the church will keep her from reaching out to me."

Steve managed a half-smile. "I'm sorry, man. Is there anything I can do to make this workable for everyone?"

"For starters, you can keep Jonny away from my sister!"

Steve chuckled. "It would be my pleasure."

Liam looked at his friend, noting a sudden change in his demeanor.

"Oh my gosh, you like my sister!"

Steve held his hands up playfully. "Don't kill me, Boss!"

Liam smiled. "I'd be honored to have you as a brother-in-law someday. You're a good Christian man. But that is up to my sister."

Steve shook his friend's hand. "I appreciate that. I feel like she's been giving me the signal that it's okay to talk to her. Is that okay with you?"

Liam felt his eyes bulge. "Really? I wouldn't have ever thought she would consider an *Englischer*. I wonder if she took the baptism. I imagine she felt she had to after I left."

Steve leaned up against the buggy. "Do you regret leaving?"

"I'm not sure I regret leaving, but I do regret not keeping in touch with my family. I shouldn't have run off without talking to my mother about it. At the time, I thought I had no other choice. I was just a dumb kid."

Steve wiped his brow and moved into the shade of the tree that the horse was tethered to. "It's not too late to change things. You should say this stuff to your mom. There is no shame in admitting you made a mistake. Family is blood and will accept each other no matter what. Your mother seems like a very kind woman. I bet she'd understand. Like you said, you were just a kid."

Liam remained quiet, processing Steve's statement. Could it really be that easy? Truth be told, Liam was terrified his mother would turn her back on him. They no longer shared the same faith. But faith was a choice; family was a given.

Chapter 11

Liam realized the only way to figure out if his mother would accept him back into her life would be to wait it out and see how they interacted during the renovation. Only time would tell if reconciliation was possible. For now, there was one more thing he had to do; he had to go next door to the bakery and see if it was indeed *his* Lucy who worked there. If it was her, he could start his apologies with her and see how it went from there. If she received him, chances were good that his family would too.

Standing to the side of the door out of view, Liam took in a few deep breaths preparing himself to enter the bakery. What was he so afraid of? Was it more concern over the possibility of her being married, or was it fear that she would reject him? He knew he still loved her, he always would. But if she'd forgotten him and moved on with her life, he would have a tougher time accepting it and living with the mistake he'd made in leaving her so long ago.

The bells on the door jingled as he opened it slowly. There was no mistaking Lucy's blue eyes and blond hair as she turned to face him. Liam nearly froze in place, mesmerized by the soft, inviting look in her eyes that used to make him weak in the knees. It was odd that she should still have that effect on him. Her eyes cast downward to the box of cookies she was filling for a customer. Liam held back pretending to look at the selection in the glass-front case. He recognized some of Lucy's signature delicacies. He wasn't surprised she was now making a living from her baking skills. He remembered the times she used to surprise him with her newest creation when they were sweethearts. He was always happy to be her taste-tester.

As Liam watched Lucy interact with the *Englisch* customer, he realized she had fulfilled her dream without leaving her family or the Amish ways. Why had he felt that leaving home was the only way to succeed? Had his desire to be like the *Englischers* been more important to him at the time? Being an *Englischer* had not been what he'd expected. He'd thought it meant total freedom, but it hadn't. Being an *Englischer* was not without its own set of problems. Now that he was where he thought he wanted to be in life, all he could think about was going back to the Amish ways.

With the customer's order filled, Lucy looked up into the handsome *Englischer's* face. "May I help you?"

Liam wanted to say so much to her, but all he could manage was to point to the special she had written on the small chalkboard to the side of the counter.

A dozen cookies? What am I going to do with a dozen cookies? Why can't I say what I came in here to say?

Lucy stood at the counter, tongs in hand, staring at Liam. How long had she been staring?

"Would you like all the same or an assortment?"

Liam cleared his throat. "Assortment, please."

Lucy took her time selecting the cookies, allowing him ample time to speak up, but he just couldn't force the words from his brain to his lips. She was more beautiful than he'd remembered her, and all he could do was stare at her. Had she been that beautiful the night he'd left her? His heart fluttered behind his ribcage, and he felt a bead of sweat roll between his shoulder blades and down his spine.

When she finished filling the box, Lucy placed it on top of the glass case, uttering his total. Liam handed her a ten-dollar bill, picked up the cookies and left the store without waiting for his change. More than that, he hadn't said another word to Lucy.

Outside in the warm summer air, Liam tried to catch his breath, but the sun seemed to steal the air from his lungs. How could she have such an effect on him? He was a grown man. But not grown up enough to apologize, he guessed.

Lucy couldn't believe Liam was walking out of her bakery without so much as a friendly word to her. Had she meant that little to him, that he couldn't even acknowledge her? The very fact he'd left her seven years ago without a second thought gave her the answer she sought. It wasn't what she wanted from him, and she wasn't willing to settle for it. She'd allowed him to leave too easily when they were teenagers, but she was a grown woman now, and capable of speaking her mind. If there was one thing Lucy did not fear, it was confrontation.

Lucy yanked on the tie to her white kitchen apron and slapped it on the counter. She had no customers to deal with, and dealing with Liam's inconsiderate behavior was at the forefront of her agenda. She would wait for the construction workers to leave for lunch, and then she would march over to the quilting shop and confront Liam. He would not get away that easily this time.

Chapter 12

Liam stepped inside the quilt shop, wondering if he would be able to face his own mother after the disaster he'd just encountered with Lucy. He evened his breath and mentally washed Lucy from his thoughts, hoping it would help him concentrate. His heart raced as he approached his mother and sister, who were looking over the supply list with Steve. He paused before interrupting, noting the mutual admiration between his sister and his best friend.

It made him happy that his sister was interested in Steve. In Liam's opinion, there was no one he would rather see Lydia with than his friend. Steve was a good man, and would do right by her. But would their mother allow such a thing? He had no doubt that Steve would convert for Lydia, but with all the negative things he'd said over the years, he wondered how eager Steve would be to succumb to the Amish ways.

Liam's thoughts went back to Lucy. Did he love her enough to go back to being Amish? Did he love his family that much? The answer was a resounding yes, but he feared it was too late.

Steve looked up at him. "Are you going to share that box of goodies, or do you plan on eating them by yourself?"

Liam knew his friend was teasing him, but he suddenly felt uncomfortable. He handed the box of baked goods over to Steve and watched him open it. Did he dare taste the sweet confections made by the hands of the woman he loved? He didn't think he could enjoy her pastries without feeling guilty, especially after the way he'd just handled himself. He'd acted no better than he had when he was a teenager.

Steve clamped his jaw over a sweet treat after offering the women first pick. He held the box out to Liam but he refused. Liam used the excuse that it was too close to lunch time even though he had no appetite at the moment. He was looking forward to the break from having to be polite to his family most of the morning while they worked. His mother had kept her distance, but he'd felt her gaze upon him several times. Liam didn't wonder where he'd inherited his stubbornness from. His mother would let him sweat it out until he came to her. It was her way; had been ever since he could remember.

Nellie asked Steve to show her the plans for renovation, leaving Liam standing alone with Lydia.

She swallowed the last bite of her cookie and leered at her twin brother. "Are you ashamed of us?"

The question startled Liam, who had immediately stuck his nose in the supply list, hoping to buy some time while coming up with something to say to his sister.

"No. Why would you ask such a question?"

Lydia brushed stray blond curls back into her *kapp.* "It seems you want to keep it a secret that you know us—that we are *familye.*"

Liam looked into his sister's eyes that burned with anger. "Steve went to school with me. He knows who you are. The rest of my crew doesn't know my past. Not because I'm ashamed of it, but because I don't talk about my personal life."

Lydia poked her brother in the arm. "Why do you think *mamm* opened this shop? She was selling her quilts fine at the flea market. She didn't need to take on a project of this stature. She did it hoping to bring you back into our *familye.* You are bringing shame on her by not acknowledging her."

Liam grabbed a cookie out of the bakery box and bit into it. It was a guilty pleasure he'd tried to deny himself, but now it was more of a distraction than the treat he'd hoped for.

"I suspected she'd opened the shop with me in mind to do the repairs. But I can't change who I am now. Too much time has passed. What do you think the Bishop will say if he finds out she's keeping company with a member of her family who rejected the baptism to become an *Englischer*? She needs the community and its support, and trying to mend fences with me could weaken that support for her."

Lydia took a deep breath. "She needs you more than she needs the community. We have not been much of a part of the community since—not since *daed's* accident and you left us. I haven't taken the baptism yet."

"You haven't?" Liam was shocked.

"*Nee.* I didn't want to and *mamm* hasn't forced it on me. I think she's afraid that if she does I will leave her like you did."

Liam ran his fingers through his dark blond hair. "I'm sorry for leaving the way I did, but at the time I was an emotional kid and didn't think it through. By the time I realized it was a mistake, it was too late to turn back."

Lydia placed her hand on his. "It's never too late to come home. We miss you."

Liam pulled his sister into a hug, and fought the tears that formed behind his eyes. "I've missed you both so much. But I had a tough time dealing with the accident. It was my fault he died. I should have been there to save him."

Lydia pulled away from her twin. "It was not your fault. If you'd been there, *mamm* would more than likely be mourning your death too."

"Hasn't she already mourned the loss of her son all this time?" Liam couldn't hold in the tears any longer. He lowered his head to disguise his pain.

"I suppose she has," Lydia said quietly.

"I've really made a mess of this haven't I?"

Lydia sniffled. "It doesn't have to be a mess. You can fix it."

"I don't think I know how."

Lydia looked him firmly in the eye. "You can start by taking responsibility for the wrong you've done. We are ready to forgive and forget, but first you have to be repentant of the sins you committed against your *familye.*"

Liam knew it was the right thing to do, but he didn't know how to give up being an *Englischer*.

Chapter 13

Lucy pulled on the front door to the quilt shop, spotting Liam toward the back of the long room. She slammed the door, watching bits of plaster filter down from the holes in the ceiling. She chided herself, knowing how hard Nellie had worked at cleaning the floor near the front of the shop. She'd have to make it up to her later. For now, her target was Liam, who'd stopped in his tracks when she slammed the front door. Now, he watched her approach, fear in his eyes the way an animal looks just before the conclusion of the hunt. She almost enjoyed the fear she saw in his eyes as she approached him, fists on her hips. When she closed the space between them, he flinched.

"Are you going to slap me again?" he asked, holding his arms in front of him defensively.

The grim line of Lucy's mouth broke when her lips parted to speak. "I should! How dare you come into my bakery after all these years and not say a word to me."

Liam backed up a step. "I had intended to say a lot of things, but I couldn't force myself to say them. I figured you've moved on with your life and probably have a family of your own and wouldn't care what I had to say anyway."

Lucy looked into his blue eyes that used to delight her when she gazed upon them. Now all she saw was a handsome stranger in front of her. She longed for him to pull her into his arms and whisper that everything was going to be alright, but it wasn't, and she couldn't allow herself to hope for such a childish whim.

"Just because I've moved on with my life doesn't mean I don't want to know where you've been all these years."

She wouldn't tell him she didn't have a husband or *kinner;* she wouldn't let him off the hook that easily. Besides, she didn't want him knowing the truth. She'd held out hope for his return all these years and had wasted that time wishing for something that would never come to pass.

"There isn't much to tell," he admitted with the pain of realization that the last seven years had been devoid of what he'd had with her. He'd taken her for granted, and he'd had to live with that regret all this time.

"There isn't much to tell?" she asked through gritted teeth. "You're an *Englischer.* Look at you. I barely recognize you anymore."

Liam heard creaking above him as he mindlessly watched bits of plaster dust float to the floor like dry, powdery snow.

"You knew when I left the community I intended to explore the *Englisch* ways. I may look like an *Englischer* on the outside, but in my heart, I will always be Amish."

It was the first time he'd really thought about it, but he'd meant every word of it. He didn't feel *Englisch* at all, despite his physical appearance. His heart would always be with his family—with Lucy. So why had it taken him this long to realize it? He wanted to pull her into his arms and tell her he still loved her, but it was obvious she had a family of her own now.

Lucy took a step toward him. "You can't have a foot in both worlds. You made a choice when you left the community, and now you will have to live with that choice."

Liam scoffed at her. "I don't have a foot in both worlds. And that decision doesn't have to be set in stone."

Lucy narrowed her eyes. "You're right. You are fully *Englisch.* You made the choice."

Liam was very aware of her every move. Her skirts wavered from the slight breeze blowing in the building from the open back door. The air around her seemed almost animated as it swirled up the plaster dust that fell from the ceiling. How could he make her understand why he'd stayed away for so long when he didn't even understand it himself? It was too late.

He'd destroyed his relationship with his family *and* with her.

Liam lifted his hands in surrender. "You're right. I can't live in both worlds, but I don't know how to go back. Too much time has passed already. Our lives have changed. We're grown up and have separate lives no matter where I stand."

Lucy studied him for a moment. Was he talking about the two of them *or* his family?

"You can go home any time you want, but you can't have it both ways."

Liam turned his back on Lucy. "I've disappointed everyone I care about. I can't do the same thing to these men that depend on me for a job. It's too late for me to go home. This is my life now whether I like it or not."

Lucy spoke softly around the lump forming in her throat. "I imagine your *mamm* would see it differently than you do."

Liam whipped around to face her. "What about you, Lucy? How do you see things?"

A single tear rolled down her cheek and she flicked it angrily. "It no longer matters what I think. Too much time has passed for us. But time stood still for your *mamm*. She's been waiting for you all this time. It's *her* time. She deserves to have her son return to her."

Lucy gazed upon his handsome face. She couldn't admit it to him that she herself had waited all these years hoping and praying for his return. The sense of betrayal would not allow her to admit she would always love him. Looking at him now was like looking into her past. He was her past and he needed to remain there for the sake of her heart. If she allowed him into her fragile heart again, it would surely break beyond repair.

Liam reached out to her, but she backed away.

"I'm sorry," he managed softly.

"Please don't come into the bakery anymore. It's best if we don't see each other anymore."

The ceiling creaked while fresh clumps of plaster fell all around Liam. Lucy turned and walked toward the open back door. Before she reached the entrance that led out to the alley, she turned to look at Liam once more, determined it would be the last time she laid eyes on him. The truth was it hurt too much to see him, and she needed to get over him once and for all.

Chapter 14

Lucy stood in the doorway of the quilt shop watching helplessly as a large portion of the ceiling collapsed onto Liam. Her feet remained planted in place as though frozen for what seemed like several minutes, when in reality only a few seconds had passed. Rushing to his side, she coughed from the cloud of plaster dust that had camouflaged the severity of the damage.

Tears clutched Lucy's throat as she tugged at a large board that had connected with Liam's head, but she couldn't budge the large section of ceiling under which he was trapped, that she estimated to be about ten feet wide. He groaned from the pain, and Lucy was grateful to hear he still had some life in him, though he lay motionless on the floor in the pile of rubble. She prayed frantically in her mind while brushing white plaster from Liam's face.

"Liam, please wake up! Open your eyes—please! I didn't mean the things I said to you...I still love you." She pleaded with him, but he barely stirred.

Muffled ringing interrupted her immediate thoughts. It was coming from the cell phone in his shirt pocket. She lifted the phone to her ear after pressing the *talk* button.

"Help," she said weakly to the person on the other end of the line. "Liam's been hurt. The ceiling of his mother's quilt shop collapsed and I'm afraid he's dying."

"This is Steve, who am I talking to?"

Lucy remembered Steve as being one of Liam's employees.

"This is Lucy Graber, I own the bakery next to the quilt shop. Can you help me? I can't move the piece of plaster board off him. It's too large."

"I'll send an ambulance, and I'll be there in just a few minutes myself."

Lucy dropped Liam's phone on the dirty floor and picked his head up, placing it gently on her lap. She smoothed his dark blond hair and pressed the corner of her apron to the cut in his hairline that the plank of wood had created. She lightly blew the plaster dust from his eyelashes, causing them to flutter.

His lashes fluttered a few more times and his breathing seemed shallow. Lucy whispered a prayer as she continued to stroke his hair lovingly. She'd dreamed of holding him again, and now that she had him close to her, she wished the circumstances could be different. She feared she would never get the chance to tell him she still loved him. Why had she wasted time arguing with him instead of declaring her love for him?

Then another thought occurred to her. Had Lydia and Nellie gone home for the day? She'd already exposed his past to his employee when he called a few minutes before. Liam would surely never forgive her for such an act of betrayal. But how could she blame him when she hadn't forgiven him for leaving her seven long years ago.

Lucy leaned down and placed a kiss on Liam's cheek. "I forgive you," she whispered. "I've not stopped loving you. I will follow you into the *Englisch* world if that's what it takes to never lose you again. I'm sorry I didn't follow you when you asked me to when we were eighteen."

Lucy began to sob. "I could have been your *fraa*. We would have had a *wunderbaar* wedding with our *familye* and friends. We could have had at least four *kinner* by now. They would all be as beautiful as you. Our girls would have bouncing blond curls and they would sit at your feet as you read the scripture. Our boys would be strong and work hard in the barn with you mucking the stalls and milking the cows. Our *dochdern* would help me plant in the kitchen garden while you and the boys were plowing the fields for planting season. We would have *wunderbaar* meals together and I would make your favorite deserts for after. I remember how much you like my baking."

Liam stirred a little, his facial expression displaying grief. Lucy imagined he was in a lot of pain, and with the weight of the large section of plaster board that still lay across his torso, she worried his breathing would stop altogether.

Lucy hiccupped a staggered breath from crying so hard. "I promise my sweet Liam that I will spend the rest of my days with you if you hang on long enough. Your *mamm* and Lydia aren't even here. Please don't die before you can reunite with them—with me."

Liam's eyes fluttered open and closed a few times, and Lucy prayed he could see her. "Shhh," she soothed him. "Everything is going to be alright. Help is on the way."

She leaned down and kissed him again, allowing her lips to linger thoughtfully on his cheek.

"I'm so sorry for slapping you all those years ago. I wanted to hold onto you and never let you go, but you were determined to leave me. I felt helpless. I don't think I stopped crying for at least three months after you left. I kept hoping you would get a taste of the outside world and come back begging me to reconcile. But you never did. After a while, I hardened my heart and refused to let anyone in my heart. I was asked to court many times, but you were always the only one I ever wanted. You are my true love."

Liam's eyes fluttered open and remained there about a half slit. "Lucy," he managed so low, she barely heard him.

Lucy cradled his head closer to her and kissed his forehead. "I'm here, Liam. I love you. I've never stopped loving you."

Out of the corner of her eye, Lucy could see Steve standing in the doorway that led to the alley. Panic traveled through her like a lightning strike as she wondered how long he'd been standing there and how much of her one-sided conversation he'd overheard.

Chapter 15

Steve rushed into the room and knelt down beside his boss and friend. He turned to Lucy and looked at her thoughtfully. "If you help me, I think we can move this piece of plaster board without hurting him. I'm going to lift and try to shove it clear of him. I need you to try to keep him still. When I move this, he may shift and it could cause more damage."

Lucy nodded as she held tight to his free arm and cradled his head in her lap.

With one swift movement, Steve picked up on the edge of the large section of ceiling and pushed until it was clear of Liam's body. Liam groaned and tried to move, but Lucy steadied him with her free hand.

Steve knelt down and checked Liam's pulse.

"His pulse is strong so that's a good sign. But we probably should try not to move him in case anything is broken. How did he get the gash in his forehead?"

Lucy pointed to the long board she'd moved after the accident. "That hit him in the head. It was still across his head, but I moved it."

"Is he still bleeding?"

Lucy eased the pressure on his head wound noting that the blood had stopped. She smoothed out her apron not caring that it was stained with blood. In the distance, she could hear the siren from the ambulance drawing near the shop. Relief washed over her when they pulled into the alley and stopped where Lucy could see them.

Two men jumped out of the ambulance and opened the back to retrieve a stretcher. They wheeled it in next to Liam and set a big box of medical supplies next to him. Lucy tried to wriggle out from under him, but the paramedics told her to stay put to keep him stable until they could check his vitals.

"Has he regained consciousness at all?" one of them asked Lucy.

"He hasn't woken up, but he's groaned a few times. He opened his eyes a few times, and I thought he looked right at me. He said my name, but he's been out for the most part."

"That's a good sign that he recognized you. Do you know him?" the paramedic asked as he looked into Liam's eyes with a small, pen-sized flashlight.

Lucy hesitated as she gazed upon Steve, but then she nodded. "*Jah,* we are old friends."

"Will you be riding with him to the hospital, Miss?" the paramedic asked.

"Someone has to tell his *familye* what happened. They don't have a phone."

Steve stepped forward. "Write down the address and I'll bring them to the hospital. You go with Liam. He needs you."

Lucy could see the sincerity in Steve's face, and it eased her worries just a little.

"I have to lock up the bakery next door. I'll be right back."

The paramedics nodded as they lifted Liam onto the stretcher. He groaned and coughed, curling and clutching at his right side. Lucy ran next door and closed the bakery and hurried out the back door into the alley, locking it behind her.

As she approached the ambulance, they were sliding the stretcher into the back. One paramedic slid into place beside the stretcher, while the other assisted Lucy into the back. He closed the doors behind her and went up front to drive to the hospital.

When they pulled into Elkhart General Hospital, Lucy realized she hadn't asked Steve to let her own *familye* know she wouldn't be home. She hoped that when her *bruder* came back to the bakery at the end of the day to pick her up that he would think she'd gotten a ride from Nellie and Lydia. She hadn't thought to leave a note on the door for him, and hoped he wouldn't worry until word could be sent home.

After the ambulance came to a stop at the emergency entrance, the driver opened the back door and assisted Lucy out first. The paramedics wheeled

Liam inside where they listed off his condition to a waiting nurse who wheeled him out of Lucy's sight.

Taking a seat in a nearby chair in the waiting room feeling unsure of what she should do, Lucy kept an eye on the set of double-doors behind which Liam disappeared. Within minutes a nurse approached her with a clipboard and asked if she could fill out the papers for Liam.

Grateful for something to do, she listed his name and birthdate along with other information she knew about him. She had thought she knew everything there was to know about him, but the fact remained that he'd been a stranger to her for the past seven years. She could easily list his history, but she had no idea what to say for anything current.

Frustrated, she put the unfinished papers in the chair next to her, staring once again at the double-doors hoping someone would invite her back to sit with Liam.

Nearly dozing off in the chair from boredom, Lucy was startled when a nurse approached her.

"Are you with the young man that was brought in by the ambulance?"

"*Jah.* Is he awake?"

"He's been mumbling the name *Lucy.* Is that you?"

Lucy nodded with downcast eyes and then followed the nurse after she took the clipboard with Liam's information on it.

"I'm sorry I couldn't fill out everything. There are a few things I don't know."

The nursed waived her off. "Don't worry about it. As long as we have his name, we can get the rest later when he wakes up."

"Is he going to be alright?" Lucy was almost afraid of the answer.

"We'll know more when we get the results of his x-rays. But for now, he's stable."

Lucy wasn't sure if that was good news or not, but as long as he was still breathing, she would be thankful.

Chapter 16

Lucy stood in the doorway of the room where they had Liam. His chest was exposed and he had wires connected to little round discs. She had seen the same things on her mother when she'd been in the hospital having surgery on her gallbladder. She also knew that the tubing in Liam's nose was feeding him oxygen.

"Don't be afraid to talk to him," the nurse urged her. "It might help to wake him up if he hears a familiar voice.

The nurse pulled a chair over to Liam's bedside and invited her to sit. She wasn't sure how much good her voice would do to help stir Liam from his slumber, but she was willing to give it a try. It seemed to keep him slightly alert while at the quilt shop just after the ceiling collapsed onto him.

Lucy sat down in the chair, unsure of what to do. She was grateful when the nurse excused herself after telling her that she would be right outside at the desk if Liam should need anything. She reassured Lucy that they were monitoring Liam from there, which made her feel a little more at ease.

Lucy stared at Liam; his torso exposed to the waste. His chest was quite sculpted compared to the way he looked when she knew him as a teenager. His arms were taught with muscles and his skin was smooth except for the occasional scratch in his skin. Bruises had risen to the surface of his skin around his ribcage, and she suspected he'd suffered a few broken ribs. She recalled her brother having the same discoloration when he'd broken three ribs after a fall from the loft in the barn when they were kids.

Lucy slipped her hand into Liam's warm hand. It still fit nicely, sending a spark of exhilaration down her spine. The cut in his hairline had strips of tape over it, but no one had cleaned the bloodstains from his cheek. She rose from the chair, reluctantly letting Liam's hand drop, and went over to the sink and pulled paper towels from the dispenser. She wet them and stepped over to Liam, wiping his face clean.

"Now this is something I imagined doing as your *fraa*. Not that I've imagined having to mop up blood from your face. But I always thought I would take care of you when you were ill. It's what I'd wanted to do since the first day I laid eyes on you."

Liam didn't stir, so she went on.

"I can't believe I've loved you since I was fifteen years old. Ten years is a long time to love a *mann* when you're not his *fraa*."

That statement seemed to get a reaction out of him. He stirred but didn't open his eyes.

"Lucy," he managed with a weak voice.

She tossed the wet towels in the trash and stood at his bedside. "I'm here. Can you open your eyes?"

She lowered herself to the edge of the bed despite the inner voice telling her she shouldn't be so brazen. But she just couldn't help herself. She was so drawn to him and longed to be near him that she didn't care what it looked like. She still loved him, and they had lost a lot of time. If something happened to him and he didn't survive this accident, she'd never be able to live with herself if she didn't at least try to win him back.

Lucy pulled his hand into hers. She admired the lines of his muscles that defined his chest as she watched him breathe. It was comforting to her that his hand was warm, because to her, that meant he was still with her. She couldn't leave his side. She feared that if she blinked he would leave her.

Liam's face seemed serene, as though he was deep in a good dream. She hoped it was so. She hated the thought of him being in pain.

Why hadn't she gone after him all those years ago? He'd offered to marry her and take her with him, but she'd turned him down without a second thought. If she had it to do all over again, she surely would say yes if given another chance.

Gott, please give me another chance with Liam. I love him. I've never stopped loving him, but you already know that. Please don't let me lose him all over again. Breathe life into his body.

Her prayer seemed selfish, she knew, but it was all she could think about. She needed him to recover so she could tell him she still loved him. Now that she was faced with the possibility of losing him again, she couldn't bear it.

Lucy felt Liam's hand close gently over hers. Her heart quickened its pace at the thought of him reaching out to her and connecting with her.

"Liam, can you hear me? It's me, Lucy. I'm here for you. Please wake up."

"Lucy." He coughed and then groaned from the pain. "I thought you were mad at me."

Lucy stared at Liam, who hadn't opened his eyes. Was he dreaming, or was he talking to her? Either way, talking *had* to be a *gut* sign—wasn't it?

"I'm not mad at you anymore. I forgave you a long time ago."

Liam tried to move, but winced from the pain, his eyelids fluttering. "But—our fight last night. You slapped me."

Lucy was confused. Had the bump on his head caused him to be disoriented? They had just fought about two hours ago, and though she'd threatened to slap him, she hadn't.

"Liam, I didn't slap you. I'm sorry for yelling at you, though."

Liam reached a hand to his eyes and rubbed them. "*Jah,* you slapped me when I told you I was leaving you to start a new life as an *Englischer.*"

Chapter 17

Lucy's heart skipped a beat. Was he delirious from the accident, or did Liam really think that their argument they'd had seven years ago had happened just last night?

"Liam, please open your eyes," Lucy said impatiently.

His eyelids fluttered. "Everything is blurry. Where am I?"

Liam squinted against the bright fluorescent lights of the emergency room.

"You're at the hospital. Do you remember what happened?"

Lucy didn't want to say too much before she gave him a chance to wrap his mind around being in the hospital. He *had* to know he was hurt, didn't he?

Liam tried to sit up, but quickly laid back down, groaning and clutching his bruised ribs.

"Where's *mei mamm* and *daed?*"

Lucy's heart caught in her throat when she heard him ask for *both* his parents. Had he blocked out the last seven years? How could she break the news to him that his *daed* had died so long ago? Perhaps it was best to avoid the question for now and give Liam a chance to wake fully. Not only was he not making any sense, but he was talking the way he used to when they were young. He spoken like and *Englischer* when they'd argued earlier.

"Steve went to your *haus* to get your *familye.*"

Liam placed a hand over his eyes to shield the bright lighting in the room. "How do you know Steve?"

Lucy knew she needed to tread lightly on her answers until he remembered where he was in terms of time. She guessed he had a concussion, and his full memory would return as soon as he gained his bearings.

"Steve is your friend from school. He was there when the boards fell on you. Don't you remember anything about your accident?"

"My head is pounding and it hurts to open my eyes. I'm surprised you're still speaking to me after our fight."

Lucy was confused. If he thought their fight was the previous night, why didn't he remember his *daed* was gone? His *daed* had died a month before their big fight. Lucy decided to play along to see just how much he remembered—at least until the nurse returned.

"I changed my mind. I decided I would very much like to be a part of your life as an *Englischer.* "

Liam lifted her hand to his and kissed it. "I'm so happy to hear that. I want so much to have my own business one day and build houses. You'll see; we will have a *gut* life together."

Lucy knew she had to be careful or she would buy into the dream that Liam had so colorfully laid out for the two of them. In reality she felt it was too late for them. But she did still love him, and wondered if that would be enough. Would he be angry with her when he regained his bearings and remembered where they were in their lives, or would he be happy for another chance to start over with her?

"What about your *familye?* "

"*Mei dead* already knows I'm going to school. He promised he would be at my graduation next month. *Mei mamm* will come around to the idea. He told me he was going to talk to her about coming with him."

Why didn't he remember about his *daed's* accident? It seemed odd that he should remember their argument, but thought that it had taken place a month earlier than it had. Lucy guessed that explained why he still thought his *daed* was still alive. She decided she should test him.

"Liam do you know what month it is?"

He tried to open his eyes again, but winced with pain. "I know I hit my head; I can feel it. But I know it's May because I'm graduating next month.

I'll be eighteen the day after I graduate and we can be married then."

He thinks he's still seventeen years old! What is he going to think if he sees me? I've aged in the last seven years! What if he doesn't like what he sees? What if he thinks I'm too old? Gott, I know this isn't kind, but please keep Liam's vision blurry until his memory is intact.

Lucy knew it wasn't right to pray for such a selfish thing, but she feared losing him again. But when his memory came back, would he remember that he no longer loved her? The situation seemed almost hopeless, but Lucy was determined to hold onto whatever tiny shred of hope she could cling to.

Liam squeezed her hand. "You're being very quiet. Am I worse off than you're telling me?"

Lucy giggled nervously. "Everything is going to be fine, Liam. You just need some rest."

"I hope you're right because I can't miss the last few weeks of school or I won't graduate. *Daed* is so proud of me. I don't want to let him down."

Lucy never realized just how supportive Liam's *daed* had been as a willing party to his attendance at the public school. She'd assumed all these years that Liam had been rebellious, and that was why he'd left the community. Was it possible that he'd had his father's blessing in all of it? Why then, did he seem so rebellious after his *daed* died? Why had he left so late at night after leaving his *mamm* a note? Perhaps he was hurting more than Lucy had given him credit for at the time. Was it possible that was the reason he was now blocking out the accident that took his father's life?

Liam tried to shift on the narrow emergency room bed. He groaned from the pain. "You're being quiet again. You haven't changed your mind about marrying me have you?"

Lucy cupped his cheek lovingly. "Of course not. I love you. I've always loved you."

It wasn't a lie even though it felt like one. She hadn't stopped loving him, but she feared he'd stopped loving her a long time ago.

Chapter 18

Lucy sat in the waiting room while more tests were being run on Liam. She was also waiting for Nellie and Lydia so she could fill them in on what was happening with Liam. The nurse had advised her that the loss of memory and blurry vision was usually temporary, but she feared she would have to continue the charade indefinitely if he didn't heal. But would that really be so bad? It might seem a little like taking advantage of a sick *mann,* but it might also be a way to get back together with Liam, and Lucy was pretty sure that was what she wanted. After all, it was what she'd been dreaming of for the past seven years. So why was she suddenly apprehensive?

If only there was a way to know if his sudden declaration of love for me was coming from his heart now, or only from his memories of the past.

Gott, please heal Liam's body and mind. Help him to remember me and his familye. Spare him the pain of learning all over again that his daed is no longer with us. Give his mamm and Lydia the strength to forgive him for the past and help him put his life back together now. I need strength too, so that I am able to let go of the past. If it is your will, please reconcile Liam with his familye—and with me.

Lucy looked at the clock on the wall of the waiting room. She was certain that her *familye* would be getting ready for the evening meal. Within an hour, she would be expected at home. She wanted to stay at the hospital, but wasn't sure if her *daed* would still be in the barn to hear the phone if she called to let him know where she was. Deciding it was worth a try, Lucy went to the nurse's desk to ask if she would allow her to make a call.

Luckily, her *daed* answered on the third ring. His stern voice practically insisted she come home, but when Lucy firmly refused his offer to send her *bruder* to pick her up, understanding changed his tone. Lucy was a grown woman, capable of making her own decisions, but she knew her *daed* still wanted to hold onto his *dochder* a little longer.

Lucy returned to her seat in the waiting room feeling discouragement settle in her heart. Her thoughts were muddled with conflicting thoughts, and none of it made any sense to her. A few hours ago she had told Liam she never wanted to see him again, but just minutes ago she was declaring her love for him all over again. Was Liam the only one that was confused? The difference was that she hadn't hit her head. She had no excuse for her behavior. It was all a lie—or was it?

The truth was a scary thing for her to admit, but she knew in her heart she could never love another *mann* as long as she drew breath into her lungs. Liam was the one her very soul yearned for. If she was capable of loving another, she'd have her own *familye* by now, but she could never bring herself to accepting the affections of any other suitor—and there had been plenty who'd called on her after Liam left. She had never been able to look beyond the love she held so dear in her heart for the one *mann* who'd betrayed her. She suddenly wondered if he'd remained as faithful to her all these years as she had been to him. Was it possible that Liam had experienced the love of another woman while living as an *Englischer*?

The very thought of it boiled her blood. It roiled in her stomach like fire. She'd made a fool of herself declaring love for a *mann* she hadn't seen for seven long years. He was as *Englischer,* capable of betraying her in the worst way. Sudden panic seized her thoughts, sending her fleeing to the restroom.

Locking the door behind her, she studied her reflection in the mirror. Small crinkles stretched from the corners of her eyes, her cheeks and nose peppered with light freckles. There was no doubt that she had aged since the last time Liam had seen her. Was it any wonder he didn't speak to her when he'd entered her bakery earlier? She'd seen how beautiful the *Englisch* women looked with their makeup to hide the flaws, and eye powders that brought out the color in their eyes better. She looked plain and simple compared to the women that frequented her bakery. Why would

Liam choose to stay true to her when he was handsome enough to get the attention of any of those women who were much more beautiful than she was?

Tears welled up in her eyes, bringing anger to her heart. So far she had refused the baptism, and it had caused a rift between her and her parents. They knew that the reasons for her rejection of the baptism and of the suitors who'd made their intentions known to her was because of her love for Liam. They hadn't pushed her, for fear she would run off to find Liam. But she knew she couldn't put it off much longer. She was nearly twenty-five years old, and it was only a matter of time before she would be expected to make the commitment or leave home. Unfortunately, she wasn't prepared to do either at this time.

Turning on the faucet, Lucy dipped her hands in the cool water and splashed it on her heated cheeks. The next handful washed over her swollen eyes. A few more splashes and she would feel better—she hoped.

Looking at her reflection again, she pulled several paper towels from the holder on the wall next to her. As she wiped her face, she wondered if she could overlook such an offense. If Liam had betrayed her with another woman sometime in the past seven years, could she take him back? Was he capable of such an act of betrayal? He certainly hadn't made any attempt to contact her. Perhaps he was perfectly happy in the *Englisch* world.

Chapter 19

Lucy finally left the restroom feeling more discouraged than when she'd gone in. Why had she refused her *daed's* prompting to send her *bruder* to bring her home? Now she was stuck at the hospital, and would have to wrestle with her conflicting feelings in front of Nellie and Lydia. How could she go back into Liam's room when he thought they were still in love? How could she continue to pretend that the last seven years apart had not occurred? If he had found love with another woman in that amount of time, he didn't show it, but that didn't mean it hadn't happened.

Gott, please show me what to do. I don't want to hurt Liam, but I don't want to get hurt either. Please spare our hearts from being broken further from this mess. I love him, Gott, I do. But I don't know if I could forgive him if he's betrayed me with the love of another woman. Please bring this to light before my heart is invested too deeply in Liam again.

Outside of Liam's room, Lucy heard a doctor trying to coax him into remembering the correct date. She felt bad for him as he struggled. Thankfully, the doctor didn't confuse him further by revealing Liam's mistake. Deciding it was best to leave Liam in the capable hands of the doctor, Lucy went back to the waiting room to wait for Nellie and Lydia. What could possibly be taking them so long to arrive? Perhaps Steve had a little trouble finding their farm.

Before she had too much time to think about it, the two women walked into the emergency room with Steve close behind them.

Nellie rushed to her side. "How is my *buwe?*"

Lucy's throat constricted at the distress on Nellie's face. "He's awake, but he's disoriented."

Relief washed over Nellie's face, and Lucy hated to give her worse news, but she figured it was better coming from her than from a stranger.

"Liam's vision is a little blurry and he is having trouble with his memory. The doctor said it was usually temporary, but he has lost the last seven years. Liam thinks he's still only seventeen—and he was asking for his *daed.*"

Nellie covered her mouth to stifle the sobs that tried to escape. Lucy placed a comforting hand on her shoulder, but the woman drew strength back into her expression and raised her chin defiantly.

"Perhaps this is *Gott's* way of giving us a second chance with him."

Nellie was right.

This Liam loved her, and when he regained his memory, there was a *gut* possibility that he would retain that love in his heart for her. It was the second chance she'd asked for, and it was up to her to put the past behind them and leave it there.

Lydia stepped forward. "Where is he? I need to see *mei bruder*. The last two conversations I've had with him were not full of kind words, and I'd like to remedy that."

Guilt had filled Lydia during the ride over to the hospital to the point she couldn't even enjoy being pressed up against Steve in the cab of his truck. She'd wanted to savor the moment of closeness with Steve, but all she could think about were the harsh words she'd spoken to Liam.

Nellie walked over to an empty corner of the waiting room. "I need to sit for a moment before I go in and see him. You go ahead and visit with him, Lydia. I'll be along after I gather my thoughts."

Lydia and Steve followed Lucy through the double doors to where Liam rested.

Nellie sat down with a thud. She felt as though the wind had been stricken from her lungs. Memories of her husband's accident rushed through her mind as she steadied herself on the waiting room chair. What had been seven long years ago seemed suddenly like it was only yesterday that she had sat in this very room while she waited to hear the news that her husband had not survived the accident. She hadn't even had the chance to tell him goodbye.

Now as she contemplated the outcome of her son's accident, she felt paralyzed with fear. How could she go in there and tell her son all over again that his *daed* was no longer with them? How could she break his heart like that a second time? The last time she'd told him he ran from her. Would he do the same thing all over again? They'd just found each other after being apart too long, and Nellie wasn't willing to lose her son again so soon.

Gott, bless me with the words to tell my son that his daed is with you. Spare his heart from breaking, and give him the strength to endure this news a second time. Preserve my familye, and help us to use this trial to bring us closer together. Preserve Liam's memories and return them to him so that he can be strong in your word. If this is your way of blessing us with a second chance to reconcile our familye, then guide us to use this opportunity wisely.

Nellie rose from the chair determined to take care of her son no matter what the outcome.

Chapter 20

Nellie stiffened her jaw and swallowed down her fear as she neared her son's hospital room. She told herself as she set her gaze upon him that the important thing was that he was still with her. She had to hold onto that in order to get her through. She'd spoken to the doctor and knew what she was up against. She would do as he instructed and keep the news of his *daed* from him for the time-being. The doctor had stated that added stress could cause him to revert further into his past memories. She certainly didn't want to be the cause of her son having a mental breakdown.

It wouldn't be easy to keep the truth from Liam, but she had taken the time to put together a reasonable excuse for why her husband was not with her. She only hoped her son would accept it.

Nellie stood in the doorway of Liam's room and took a deep breath, pasting a smile on her face. It didn't matter that her son probably couldn't see her smiling, but it helped to ease the pain in her aching heart. She was almost grateful that her son's vision would be blurry for a while, as she worried he would be shocked at how much she had aged over the past seven years.

Stepping quietly into the room, she moved slowly toward Liam's bedside. His ribs were bruised and his head was red and swollen near his hairline. The steady whirring sound from the oxygen that streamed into his nose through narrow tubing filled the room. Nellie hated awkward silence, and was grateful for the little bit of noise the oxygen provided. The room smelled strongly of disinfectant, and Nellie fought to keep her stomach from retching. A monitor to the side of the bed beeped repetitiously with every beat of her son's heart, and the sound was comforting to Nellie. It meant that her son was breathing and his heart was strong. Something she'd always taken for granted—until now.

Nellie lowered herself carefully into the chair beside the bed, trying not to intrude on her son's slumber. She was content with watching him breathe, even though she was eager to see him awake. Her maternal instincts urged her to lift the covers over Liam to protect him from the chill in the room, but she opted not to disturb him.

Though he'd cut his thick blond hair short to mimic the styles of the *Englisch,* Nellie could still see the strong resemblance to his *daed* when she looked at Liam. She'd fallen in *lieb* with Liam's *daed* because of the same rebellious streak she noted their son had inherited. How could she fault him for growing up to be so much like his *daed*? If not for his love for Nellie and his eagerness to marry her, her husband wouldn't have taken the baptism either. Now she was left with his two *kinner* who had taken their *daed's* rebellion a little too literally. Perhaps it was time she left the community and clung to her children. They were all she had left from her husband, and she didn't want to lose them too. Surely *Gott* would forgive her as long as she held fast to her faith.

Nellie let her thoughts drift to the day Liam and Lydia were born. The pregnancy had been almost unbearable, and would have done her in if not for her husband doting on her the way he had. She remembered the proud look on her husband's face when Liam was born first. She hadn't been aware she was carrying twins, and had felt a little disappointment until she saw the admiration in his *daed's* eyes. Then when the pains intensified once more, she feared something was wrong until the midwife had presented her with her *dochder*.

Then after, when they'd rushed her to the hospital after her uterine wall had ruptured, she nearly lost her life. Her husband was by her side the entire time, while her *schweschder* filled in as wet-nurse for her twins. She recalled how supportive her husband had been when he learned she could have no further *kinner*.

Their *familye* had survived many trials over the years, but the death of her husband had unraveled them. Now that is was up to her, she would weave her *familye* back together no matter how much work it presented. She would make certain her son knew how much she loved him, and how much he was wanted back home where he belonged.

Liam stirred, bringing Nellie out of her reverie. *"Mamm?"*

It was a simple word, but it meant the world to her to hear that from his lips. It wasn't the polite Ma'am that it had been only yesterday. Now it was the term of endearment she hadn't heard from him for seven long years.

Nellie stood up, placing her hand protectively over her son's.

"I'm here."

A slight smile tipped the corners of his mouth.

"Where's Lydia and *Daed?"*

Nellie's lips narrowed as she swallowed hard. This was it. She was about to lie to her son. Before she could muster up the courage to speak the words, Liam drifted back to sleep. She breathed a heartfelt prayer of thanks that she didn't have to say the words just yet. She knew it was only a matter of time before he woke fully and asked the question again. For now, she was in the clear.

Nellie slumped back down into the chair beside the bed, willing her heart to slow enough to catch her breath. Anxiety gripped her in a way it hadn't since the death of her husband. She wasn't ready to relive the painful memories she'd worked so hard to bury along with the *mann* she loved. If he were here with her now, he would provide her with the support she needed. For the first time since his death, she would have to rely on her own strength to get her through. It was times like this one that keeping her hands busy helped to quiet her mind. After her husband died, quilting had been the only thing to keep her idle hands from wringing with anxiety. Now, as she sat at her son's bedside, she wished for a needle and quilt squares to keep her mind and hands too busy to let worry set in.

Chapter 21

Lydia squeezed into the middle of Steve's truck once again, while Lucy sat in the passenger's side. *Mamm* had told them to go home since Liam had been transferred to a private room and had not woken up even once. He didn't even stir when the nurses had wrapped his cracked ribs. He'd groaned quite a bit, but not once did he open his eyes. The doctor told them it was normal for him to sleep a lot after what his body had been through, but the nurses continued to disturb him on the hour to be sure he wouldn't slip into a coma.

On the ride to their farm, Lydia carried on nervous small talk with Lucy about shucking corn and shelling peas. They talked about the upcoming canning bee that the women of the community would begin soon. They even discussed the excitement over the quilt shop and the plans for it once the renovations were completed. Lydia kept the conversation going as much as she could to avoid thinking about Steve, who was pressed quite close to her in the small cab of his truck. She had become smitten with Steve the first time she'd met him, and she secretly hoped he liked her too.

Since Liam had left home, Lydia had not been afforded the opportunity to have a serious beau. She was always too busy doing Liam's old chores along with her own, and most her *mamm's* usual duties. She too was overworked and overtired most days to even think about having a beau. But now, as she snuggled close to Steve, she was all too aware of what she'd been missing out on when each of her friends had gotten married one-by-one. Lucy was the only friend she had left that was still single, and the two of them threw themselves into their work to avoid the obvious emptiness they each endured on a daily basis.

Lydia had advised Lucy many years ago to stop waiting for her *bruder* to return, but the poor thing hadn't listened to her. Today, she saw the love in Lucy's eyes when they were in Liam's hospital room, and the light in her eyes had returned. Lucy had appeared happy, but Lydia could still see reservation in her expression. She imagined it had to have been tough for Lucy to pretend with Liam that they were still young, especially since that was the time in their lives when they were in love.

Chattering on, Lydia was grateful that Lucy was easy to talk to. Her *bruder* had been a fool to leave Lucy, but Lydia was content with their friendship. Their common bond had been their abandonment from Liam. It had in some ways brought them together as friends, but Lydia often wondered if their friendship was a bit strained by the pain Lucy felt in her presence at times.

Holidays had been especially difficult for all of them. When Lucy brought a gift for Lydia each year on her birthday, Lydia could tell that thoughts of Liam were in the back of Lucy's mind. Lydia knew that whatever the outcome of this new set of circumstances, they would have each other to lean on if things became tough.

They both avoided the obvious during their chatter; neither of them wanted to admit that Liam's memory lapse could actually be a blessing in disguise. Even Nellie had seemed a little curious to know how the situation could work in their favor. They were all eager to see Liam heal, but they also didn't mind the possibility that this could bring the outcome they'd all hoped for along the past seven years.

Lucy shifted in her seat and leaned against the door of the truck, watching mindlessly as the landscaping coasted by in a blur of color. Barns blended with trees and cows seemed an extension of the earth. Was Lydia going to talk the entire way home? Lucy tried politely to tune out her nervous prattling, but the girl just kept engaging her in question after question. If she knew Lydia, she was using conversation to cover up something that was weighing on her mind. Lucy had her own issues she was trying not to think about, but it was no use trying to push them down because they seemed to repeatedly surface on their own.

Lucy let her mind drift to Liam, and wondered how long it would be before he realized he didn't really love her anymore. No amount of pretending could make him love her if didn't, especially if the memories he relied on were from a time when he *did* love her. Those old feelings might be better left in the past, but Lucy couldn't push them down any longer.

How could Liam forget that he wasn't in love with her anymore? Was it possible that he'd never stopped loving her, and the accident had brought *his* feelings to the surface? The only question that still plagued Lucy was whether or not Liam had loved any other woman in the time they'd been apart. If he had, was there any real hope for them to reconcile? Was Lucy capable of forgiving such an offense, or would she spend the rest of their lives letting it eat away at her until she became so bitter that she could no longer love him? She prayed it wasn't so.

Chapter 22

"At least let me send you home with a jar of my homemade apple butter."

There was a gentle insistence in Lydia's tone that Steve could not resist.

"That sounds wonderful, thank you. I'll wait right here."

Steve knew better than to accept the invite from Lydia for a glass of iced tea on the porch. So he sat in the truck and watched Lucy disappear into the cornfield that separated her farm from Lydia's. Even though it was dusk, he could see that a wide trail had been left between the tall rows of corn. He guessed it was planted that way on purpose to allow passage between the two farms. It intrigued him how neighborly the Amish were. He'd lived that way growing up, being on a street where all the neighbors pitched in to help one another. He missed that now that he lived in the city.

Steve rolled down the window of his truck so he could listen to the crickets. The wind rustled the tassels on the corn stalks, bringing him out of his truck to get a better listen to the country sounds that captivated his attention. He was so absorbed in the charm of the land that he didn't hear Lydia step out of the front door of the farm house. A light flickered to the side of him as Lydia lit the lantern on the small table on the porch. When she beckoned him onto the porch, he resisted only for a minute. His better judgment told him Liam wouldn't approve, but Lydia's eyes hypnotized his heart just long enough to reel him in. He sat in one of the wooden chairs separated by the table that housed the lantern and the tray of iced tea that Lydia had brought out for them to share.

"I hope you don't find it too presumptuous, but when I saw you get out of your truck to admire the corn, I thought you changed your mind about joining me for a refreshing sip of iced tea."

Steve nodded to her, watching her pour the tea into tall glasses filled with slices of lemon. Soft blond tendrils fluttered against her cheek, and her eyes shone like the stars that were just beginning to light up the indigo sky. He was mesmerized by her beauty that didn't come from makeup or fancy hair or clothing like the city girls. Lydia's beauty came from within and radiated to her outer appearance like a halo. To Steve, she was the most beautiful woman he'd ever laid eyes on.

"Just a half glass for me," he said, interrupting her pouring. "Then I should be on my way. I'm not sure your brother would approve of me being here without an escort."

Lydia paused before setting the pitcher of tea back on the small table. "I'm a grown woman, and *mei bruder* hasn't been here to guide me in that process, so I'm not sure he has claim to his say about the matter."

Steve had been awkward at dating since he was a teenager. He was shy and didn't know what to say half the time, but Lydia had put him at ease from the moment he'd met her. Her smile was enough to melt his pounding heart.

"I imagine he would have a lot to say. He's still your brother, and he's never stopped loving you. I've heard so much about you over the years, I feel like I already know you."

Lydia nearly choked on her iced tea. "That hardly seems fair! You'll have to catch me up so I know an equal amount about you."

Steve cleared his throat. "That could take a while."

"The only thing I have to do right now is watch the corn grow." Lydia smiled at him.

Steve relaxed a little and smiled back. If Lydia was okay with him sitting on the porch alone with her, then he wouldn't argue. He was happy to be in her company, and Liam had all but given him his blessing earlier—before the accident.

"You know I met your brother back in ninth grade. He still lived at home back then, and it was a struggle for him. If not for the support of his dad, he wouldn't have made it to graduation."

Lydia's eyes grew wide. "I didn't know our *daed* knew he was going to the public school."

"Your dad was supposed to go to Liam's graduation, but he...didn't make it."

"Because he died in the accident," Lydia added.

"Yes," Steve said quietly. "Liam told me he was going to bring your mother to the graduation."

"*Mamm* knew about it too?" Lydia was having a hard time grasping that bit of information. "Why didn't she tell me?"

Steve didn't know what to say. He didn't want to be in the middle of this conversation or in the middle of the feud between sister and brother.

"I've found over the years that sometimes people have a tough time telling others how they really feel about things. From what I know of your brother, I'd say you all need to learn to communicate a little better. And don't think I haven't said that to *him* quite a lot since I've known him."

Lydia sighed. "Maybe Liam's accident was a blessing in disguise. Maybe now that he thinks he's back where all this started, we can have a chance to work through what went so wrong in our *familye* after *mei daed's* accident. None of us spoke to each other after the accident; we just held in our feelings about everything and went our own separate ways."

Lydia pondered her own statement as she gazed up into the sea of stars against a cobalt sky. The crescent moon hung amidst the stars as though keeping order over the vast universe. She listened to the crickets and the rustling of the corn stalks in the field as if the resonance whispered a message of hope directly from *Gott*—as if hope floated across the warm, summer breeze.

Chapter 23

Lucy stepped onto the path between the rows of corn that led to Lydia's farm. Though the sun had barely tipped over the horizon, she was to meet Lydia so the two of them could get a ride into town with Steve. She hadn't told her folks she was going to the hospital again or anything about Liam's accident because they would not understand her need to be involved. Her *familye* had lectured her repeatedly about letting go of Liam, but she had not let her heart let go of him. Now she was on her way to the hospital to see him, and she felt as nervous as a teenager again.

Reaching out a hand, Lucy tapped the leaves of the cornstalks as she whisked by them. Liam used to chase her around this very field in the summers, and they would swim in Goose Pond, and skate across it in the winter. She had a history with Liam, and now she had a chance at the future with him she'd always dreamed of. Even though it wasn't the ideal beginning to that future, she was determined to try to make it work to her advantage. She'd missed him more than she realized.

Suppressing a yawn, Lucy pressed on though the dirt under her feet was still very damp with early morning dew. She hadn't slept much, and thought about the thermos of coffee she carried, wondering if it would be enough to keep her awake all day. She'd been so consumed with thoughts of Liam, she hadn't fallen asleep until well into the wee hours. At eight o'clock now, she'd been up for two hours already doing chores to prepare for her absence from the farm for the day.

All she could think about the entire night was how she felt about leaving her *familye* and the community to cling to Liam. She was more mature than she was the first time she'd pondered the question, and she believed more than ever that she was finally ready. If that was what Liam would require of her, she would choose *him* this time. She loved him; she had never stopped.

At the clearing, Lucy could see Steve's work truck parked in front of Lydia's *haus.* Steve leaned up against the bed of the truck, his hands moving around tools in the back. The squeak of the screen door let Lucy know that Lydia had been waiting for her approach before exiting the *haus.* In her arms was a medium rucksack, and if she knew Lydia, it was packed with food for the day. Lucy hadn't thought past the thermos of coffee that she hoped would keep her awake. With food in her belly, it might be tough to fight sleep with the long day ahead of her.

After a brief greeting, she and Lydia climbed into the truck and they headed toward the hospital. The closer they got, the more Lucy's stomach roiled with second thoughts. She was so sure she'd made the right decision, but now that she was about to come face-to-face with Liam, she began to overanalyze her decision yet again.

Thankfully, Lydia didn't seem to be in a very chatty mood this morning, or Lucy would not have been able to sort out her feelings before they reached the hospital. Secure in her resolve, Lucy stepped out of the truck with confidence in knowing exactly how she would handle herself with Liam when she saw him.

Lydia already noticed a connection with Steve. Their long talk the night before had helped bring them closer together, and she was content with their friendship moving at such a fast pace. At twenty-five, Lydia was at risk of becoming a spinster according to the way most Amish viewed marriage. Most girls are married by the time they turn twenty, and Lydia had watched each of her friends marry. There was not much choice of bachelors in the community, but Lydia did not care. Her heart was already filling with hope for a future with Steve. Though she feared her *mamm* would not approve, she tried to push the thought of leaving the community the way Liam had out of her mind for the time-being. Was she prepared to leave if forced to choose? There was a part of her that was, and that frightened her enough to push down the thoughts.

Lydia took her time scooting out of the middle of the cab of the truck, enjoying the feel of the hand Steve had offered her. In her opinion, it fit perfectly. The only thing that could be more pleasant would be to have his lips meet hers. Now was not the time for that, Lydia knew, but that didn't stop her from daydreaming about that perfect moment when such a magical thing would finally happen for her. One look into Steve's blue eyes, and Lydia was certain he was thinking the same thing. She'd caught him gazing at her mouth a few times last night, and she'd hoped he would be assertive enough to give into the temptation, but he hadn't. Much to her dismay, he'd acted like the perfect gentleman.

With Lucy already ducking into the hospital entrance ahead of them, Lydia was tempted to linger outside with Steve for a few moments, but she knew her *mamm* would need the change of clothing she'd brought for her. She'd also brought a pair of her *daed's* trousers and a shirt just like her *mamm* had asked of her because Liam's clothes he'd left behind in his teens would no longer fit him. Lydia wished she'd had the time to wash the musty clothes she'd taken from the old trunk in the attic, but they would have to do for now.

Lydia and Steve ambled down the hallway to Liam's room. It was evident to her that Steve enjoyed her company, and she hoped that when Liam was well, she and Steve would have the opportunity to explore those feelings a little more in-depth. For now, she would concentrate on helping her *bruder* get back to whatever path he would take for his life. Liam had been given a fresh start whether he was aware of it yet or not, and Lydia would do everything she could to make sure she and her *mamm* were a part of his future.

Chapter 24

Lucy crept quietly into Liam's room, careful not to disturb him. She'd run into Nellie at the nurse's station, and the woman encouraged Lucy to take a turn visiting with her son while she stretched her legs.

Grateful for a few moments of privacy with Liam, Lucy sat in the chair beside the bed and pulled his hand into hers. Even in the hospital gown, Liam was adorable. She longed for him to wake so she could pull him into her arms and declare her love for him, but there would be plenty of time for that later. For now, she would be content that he had survived the accident, and that *Gott* had given them all a second chance with him.

Liam turned his head toward Lucy and opened his eyes a small slit. His vision was still blurry, but he could feel the warmth of her hand in his. He groaned as he tried to move. His ribs hurt and his head pounded.

"Don't try to get up," Lucy's gentle voice urged. "You've had an accident. Do you remember anything yet?"

He winced from the pain in his head. "The buggy accident!"

Liam tried to sit up again, but was unable due to the pain coursing through him. "Is *mei daed* here too? Is he injured?"

Tears constricted Lucy's throat. How could she tell the *mann* she loved that his *daed* had passed away seven years before?

Nellie walked into the room just then and stood at her son's bedside.

"Your *daed* is not here, Liam. He's visiting relatives."

It was enough to calm him down, but both women knew it wouldn't satisfy him for long. It wasn't exactly a lie, Nellie conveniently left out the part about it being relatives in Heaven that her husband was with. The two women looked at each other for a long moment, stress distorting their faces. They knew the real explanation would come out soon enough, but for now, Liam was content.

Unable to control her tears, Lucy excused herself abruptly and exited the room. In the hall, she let her tears flow freely. What had she been thinking when she'd decided that reuniting with Liam was a *gut* idea? It hadn't really sunk in that she would have to pretend to be seventeen again in order to keep him. What if he never regained his memory of the last seven years? Would she have to pretend to have her birthdays all over again? She'd wished so many times to have those years back, but now that she was faced with it, the concept was a little too terrifying for her to deal with.

She felt a hand on her shuddering shoulders and immediately stiffened and wiped her face. Nellie pulled Lucy into her arms allowing her to let go of a fresh batch of tears.

"I'm so sorry," Lucy sobbed. "I didn't know what to say to him when he asked me about—your husband."

"You've done a fine job of caring for him during this. I'm happy he had you here with him yesterday before I was able to get here. Thank you for helping us. You don't have to be here, but I know you are here because you love him, and I'm grateful my son has you to care for him. I've prayed that *Gott* will give the two of you another chance to make things right between you."

"Thank you," Lucy said quietly.

Lydia and Steve met them in the hall. Nellie and Lydia exchanged a strained glance between them before she handed her *mamm* the bag in her hand.

"I brought you a spare dress and *Daed's* clothing for Liam so he can wear them home tomorrow."

Lucy turned her gaze sharply until it met Nellie's. "You're bringing Liam *home* with *you?*"

"*Jah*. The doctor here said it's best if he follows a normal routine and remains in familiar surroundings to trigger his memories."

Lucy's head filled with immediate questions, but she didn't want to be disrespectful to Nellie.

Steve spoke the words she'd been thinking but didn't dare utter. "He should probably go back to his apartment in the South Bend. That would probably trigger his memories faster, wouldn't you think?"

"Nee. He believes he's still a teen, and it might be traumatic for him to find out suddenly that he'd left the community. As long as he believes his *daed* to be still alive, he needs to be at home with me and his *schweschder,* so that when his memory comes back, we will be there to comfort him through it."

Steve nodded. "That makes sense."

Lucy couldn't hold it in any longer. "He thinks he was in the buggy accident with his *daed.* He asked me about it just before you walked in the room."

Nellie sighed. "Then I suppose we will have to break the news to him a little bit at a time. We can start by taking him by the quilt shop in a few days and showing him what really happened. Maybe that will trigger something in his mind. He's going to expect to try to finish school, so Steve, you're going to have to come up with a reason he doesn't need to go anymore."

Steve nodded. "What if we just tell him that a little time has passed and he already graduated?"

"I don't want to confuse him more, but the doctor did say he needs to be brought up to the present time—but slowly. Maybe if we tell him everything a little at a time, he will come to it on his own."

They all agreed, but Lucy still had a few reservations. If he regained his memory too quickly, she feared he would remember he no longer loved her, and it would destroy their chance at a future together.

Chapter 25

Liam couldn't shake the feeling that nagged him about his apprehension over going home with his *mamm* and Lydia. He couldn't put his finger on it, but something seemed a little off about the situation. Despite reassurance from the doctors, his *familye,* and Steve, his best friend, he still felt uneasiness creeping into his mind. Was there something that his *familye* was keeping from him? Why had his *daed* taken this opportunity to visit with his relatives? Hadn't he been in the buggy accident with Liam?

Pieces of his memories were missing, and it troubled Liam to the point of exhaustion. The doctors had advised him not to try too hard to remember, reassuring him the memories would return on their own. But what if they never did? What if he never remembered what happened to him? Would it be that bad? Maybe it was better that he didn't remember his accident. But he couldn't shake the feeling everyone was keeping something important from him.

Liam had his whole life ahead of him, and Lucy had agreed to marry him and start a new life with him outside of the Amish community. It had been his dream to have his own construction business, with his best friend working side-by-side, and now it was closer than ever. All he had to do was finish his last few weeks of school and graduate, and then he would be eighteen and ready to be on his own—with Lucy, the love of his life.

ഐശ്ദ

Lucy and Lydia had remained at the Yoder farm that morning to prepare for Liam's homecoming. No matter how hard Lucy tried to stay calm, the butterflies disturbed her stomach. Why had she agreed to run off with Liam? Would he expect her to if he didn't regain his memory before he was able to leave the community? She knew he had at the very least a week of physical recovery ahead of him, but would that prevent him from pushing her to make plans with him? She wondered what would happen when he realized he already had a place of his own in the city.

Lucy pulled fresh muffins from the oven and upturned them into a linen-lined basket. Lydia had practically begged her to make them since they had always been Liam's favorites. She couldn't deny him that; she would do anything for him. Even carrying on the charade of reliving their youth was all for him—or was it? She had to admit that a part of her felt selfish for wanting another chance with Liam, even it meant he might not remember they had been split up for so long.

"Do you fear that Liam will leave us all over again when he remembers what happened and how much time has really passed?"

Lydia's question startled Lucy, who'd been lost in her own thoughts. It was a legitimate question, and one that warranted an answer, but Lucy couldn't allow herself to think about the consequences of the situation. The entire thing could backfire in their faces, but to Lucy, it was worth a try just to be near the *mann* she loved once again.

"Let's not borrow trouble, Lydia. We should remain strong in our faith and believe that the outcome will be *Gotte's Wille.*"

The very thought of leaving her future up to *Gott* terrified Lucy. She knew better than to let her faith waver, but she did not have the strength to recover from another heartbreak involving Liam, and she suspected the same was true for Lydia and Nellie.

Lydia smiled at her friend. "You're right. They will be here soon. Is there anything we forgot?"

Lucy took a mental note of all the breakfast foods that spread across the table and hoped Liam would have an appetite when he walked in and smelled the food. No sooner had she resolved they hadn't missed anything, than they heard Steve's truck pull into the drive at the back of the *haus.*

Lydia and Lucy stared at each other wide-eyed for a brief moment before busying themselves with setting the dishes on the table. Steve entered through the kitchen door with Liam leaning on him for support. Lucy pulled out a kitchen chair just in time for Steve to lower Liam into it. Groaning from the pain, Liam took a few deep breaths. Lucy rushed to the sink and wet a linen dishtowel and brought it to him, mopping up the sweat on his brow. Liam clasped his hand over hers and held the linen towel over his eyes. His hand shook as he breathed in deeply, but he didn't let go of Lucy's hand.

Feeling awkward, Lucy pulled gently to release her hand from his. "I hope you're hungry; we made you some breakfast."

"It smells *gut.* I didn't eat much at the hospital because it didn't taste like *mamm's* cooking." He removed the cloth from his eyes and pointed his blurry gaze in Nellie's direction. "Where's *Daed?* I was hoping he'd be back by now. I need to talk to him."

Silence suffocated the room.

Nellie bravely stepped forward and placed a hand on her son's shoulder. "Is it something that can wait, or can I help instead?"

"Nee. It can wait. Let's eat. I'm starving."

Lucy eyed Liam for a moment. Was it just her imagination, or had his last few sentences sounded more like an *Englischer?* If he was speaking differently, then it was possible his brain was beginning to heal, and it was only a matter of time before he realized he was no longer in love with her. Would she lose him forever, or would she have enough time to make him fall in love with her all over again? Lucy had to face the possibility that her plan might not work, and that terrified her.

Chapter 26

Lydia sat on the front porch once again with Steve. With her *mamm* and Lucy preoccupied with her *bruder,* Lydia intended to take advantage of a little time for herself to see where her new friendship with Steve would take them. He'd been invited for dinner after a long day at the quilt shop working on the renovation, and Lydia was glad for the private time they could spend getting to know one another.

Lighting the citronella buckets Steve had brought her from the hardware store in town, Lydia was grateful for his consideration in keeping away the mosquitoes. The night before when they'd sat out here, she'd gotten bitten a few times.

"It's very humid tonight," Steve said. "The mosquitoes like the humidity. Hopefully once those candles burn for a few minutes, they'll disappear and we can enjoy the night breeze again."

Lydia poured two tall glasses of iced tea, hoping the refreshing brew would keep them cool enough to sit for a while.

"How did your day go at the quilt shop?"

Steve sighed. "I'll admit it wasn't the same without your brother, but I think we managed to keep anymore of the ceiling from caving in. I think we have it all secure now. We don't need anyone else getting hurt. Liam seemed a little more alert at dinner."

"*Jah,* I think he got a lot of rest today. Maybe sleeping in his own bed again made him feel better."

"I don't blame him. It's peaceful out here. I wouldn't mind settling down in a place like this myself."

Lydia felt her heart leap against her ribcage. Was it possible her way of life was appealing enough to Steve that he would consider marrying her some day? She knew it was too soon to think such things, but she couldn't help it. She was smitten with Steve, and it seemed he was beginning to show signs he was thinking along the same path as she was.

"Most people like it better here than in the city. You can see every star out here without the city lights blocking them out. The city is much too noisy and busy."

Steve stood up and offered his hand to her.

"Let's take a look at those stars, shall we?"

Lydia felt giddiness try to overcome her as she placed her hand in Steve's and allowed him to guide her down the steps of the porch. Their hands remained clenched as they walked along the path toward the cornfield away from the canopy of trees that blocked out the sky.

Steve stopped just short of the entrance to the cornfield and turned to face Lydia. He wanted to kiss her with everything that was in him, but he put his emotions in check for fear he might be pushing things along too quickly for Lydia's comfort.

It was Lydia who closed the space between them. Now that she stood dangerously close to Steve, he couldn't resist leaning down and touching his lips to hers.

ഇ൭ൽ

Lucy breathed a sigh of relief when Nellie excused herself to retire for the night. She hadn't been alone with Liam since the day of his accident, and she was eager to spend some quality time with him. She knew she couldn't stay long because he needed his rest, but she was not ready to let him go so easily just yet. She stared at his handsome face in the glow of the lantern light that illuminated the room.

Liam smiled. "I can't believe *mamm* left us alone like this. But it doesn't matter because we will be married soon and we will have our own place in the city."

"It sounds *wunderbaar.*"

"When we become *Englischers* we will have to talk the way they do if we want to fit in. We will have to dress like them too. Are you going to be able to do that, Lucy?"

Lucy swallowed hard. She hadn't thought that far ahead. Was she willing to give up her plain clothing for clothing that wasn't modest? For Liam, she would if it meant keeping him in her life.

"*Jah.* I mean, *yes.*"

"I haven't told *mamm* about our plans yet. I was hoping to talk to *mei daed* first. I wish she would tell me when he's expected to return from his trip."

Lucy suppressed the tears that threatened to spill from her eyes, and was grateful the wick in the lantern had burned down enough to dim the room, allowing her to better hide her feelings.

"Have you decided where you want us to live?"

Lucy tried changing the subject, hoping Liam would take the bait.

Liam pushed his hand through his hair. "I had planned on getting a place with Steve, but now that you've agreed to marry me, I guess we'll have to find our own place. I have enough money saved to get us started, but I'll have to find work right away."

He ran his fingers through his hair again, feeling puzzled. "Why is my hair so short? Did they have to cut it because of the stitches in my head?"

How could she answer that without lying to him? "You are the one who cut it," she blurted out without thinking through her answer.

He slowly sat up, wincing as he maneuvered into an upright position. "Why did I cut it? To look more *Englisch?*"

"*Jah.*"

It was all she could say, but it was the truth.

"I don't want you to cut your hair," Liam said as he pulled her by her hands until she sat at the edge of his bed.

Lucy reached up and unpinned her *kapp* and set it on the bedside table. She used to pull her hair down for him all the time when they were dating, but did she dare do it now, after all these years? To him, time had not moved forward seven years, but for her, it seemed almost too much time had passed since she'd held him in her arms.

Chapter 27

Lucy woke a little later than usual feeling disappointed that she wouldn't have more than a few minutes to see Liam when she went to pick up Lydia to drive into town. Since Nellie would be staying at home caring for Liam for the next few days, Lydia offered to oversee the renovations of the quilt shop. Lucy knew the main reason she'd volunteered was so she could see Steve, but Lucy would never dream of exposing her friend's secret "crush".

Just as the sun began to show, streaking pinks and yellows across the horizon, Lucy pulled her buggy into the back side of the Yoder farm. She stepped down onto the dew-drenched grass and walked sleepily up the steps to the kitchen door. She knocked a brief warning before entering. The smell of freshly fried bacon and cinnamon rolls filled her senses. She'd left home without any breakfast, eager to get to the bakery after leaving it closed for the past two days. Her regular customers would be lined outside the door waiting on her this morning, she was sure of it, and she knew she was in for a long day. The sooner she arrived, the sooner she could be done and return to Liam at the end of her day.

Lydia was still sitting at the table, and quickly shoved the last piece of bacon in her mouth. Lucy had to smile at her friend, who could eat twice as much as she could and never gain an ounce. Lucy, on the other hand, had grown a little thicker over the past few years, and had often wondered if it was one of the reasons she was still single. It was something she had worried about when she saw Liam again for the first time after so many years, but thankfully, he'd acted like he hadn't even noticed.

"Sit and have some food. I made too much as usual."

Lucy waved her off. "*Nee.* If I'm to make a *gut* impression on your *bruder,* I need to start watching what I eat. It doesn't help that I have a habit of tasting a sample from each batch of pastries at the bakery."

"You are skin and bones, Lucy! Eat!"

Lucy didn't believe her, but she had to admit she was very hungry. She agreed to a little bit of eggs and one piece of bacon. Liam entered the room clutching his ribs just then and caused Lucy to spit eggs into her napkin. Why was she suddenly so nervous around him? They'd spent a pleasant evening together, and had even made plans for their future.

"Lydia's right. I've always thought you were too thin, Lucy. Stay for a few minutes and eat with me."

Liam smiled, and Lucy jumped up nervously to fill a plate for him. She set it front of him, feeling self-conscious about eating, so she took small bites, while Liam gobbled his food and asked for a second helping.

After a little bit of small-talk, Lydia came back into the kitchen and asked if Lucy was ready. Lucy wasn't ready to go; she wanted to stay and have things be as magical as they had been the night before, but she could sense something had changed in Liam. Was it possible that he'd remembered his real life, and he no longer wanted anything to do with her? Lucy suddenly felt like a fraud, and hoped he wouldn't end up hating her instead.

Liam wiped his mouth and tossed the linen napkin carelessly on his plate. "Where are the two of you off to today?"

The two women eyed each other for a moment, and Lucy wondered if they should tell him the truth. At his present memory level, Liam would have no idea about her bakery, since her *daed* did not present her with it until Liam had already left the community. He certainly had no recollection that his *mamm* now owned a quilt shop.

"We have a few things to take care of in town," Lydia offered. "We will be gone most of the day, but I will be back in time to help *mamm* prepare the evening meal."

Liam looked at the two of them as though he knew they were keeping something from him. "What business do the two of have in town that would keep you all day?"

He turned his attention toward Lucy. "Are you going to the bakery?"

Lucy's heart slammed against her ribcage. If he knew about the bakery, then he must remember that they were no longer together.

"*Jah*. How did you know?" she was almost too afraid to ask.

"Your *daed* gave it to you for your eighteenth birthday. But you're birthday isn't for a few more…weeks."

Lucy looked into Liam's confused expression and couldn't help but fear that he would remember at any moment that he no longer loved her, and her future with him would be over—again. Lydia tried to nudge her out the kitchen door, but Lucy's feet felt like they were nailed to the floor. Silence hovered between them until Nellie entered the room.

"You two better get going or you'll be late opening that bakery," she said sternly.

Liam turned to his *mamm*. "Have I missed something?"

Nellie shooed the girls with her hand, though they both looked worried—Lucy more than Lydia.

"You haven't missed anything. The doctor told you that you had a few things missing from your memory, but it will all come back to you in time."

"I think I'm going to head out to the barn and feed Buttercup. The doctor said the sooner I get back to my normal routine the easier I will start to remember the little things I'm missing." Liam stood up slowly.

Nellie put a hand on his shoulder. How could she tell him that his old mare had died a few years back? "You can't tend to Buttercup because you're *daed* took the horse with him."

Chapter 28

Lydia pushed Lucy out the kitchen door. She couldn't stand to be in the *haus* with her *bruder* another minute. How could her *mamm* be so casual about the dead horse, or about their dead father for that matter? Lydia knew she could never be that brave for Liam's sake. What was her *mamm* thinking telling Liam such a thing?

Lydia burst out laughing.

Lucy looked at her friend as though she'd gone mad. "What is so funny?"

Lydia could barely stop laughing long enough to answer her. "The horse is dead! And *Mamm* told Liam that *mei daed* took the horse with him!"

Lucy stifled a giggle. "It's not funny."

"I know it's not," she said. "But in a way it is."

Lucy crinkled her brow. "This is like when we were young and our *mamm's* told us to behave during Sunday service, and you know you aren't supposed to laugh, but you can't help it, so you laugh when it's inappropriate to laugh."

Lydia giggled some more. "That's it exactly!"

Lucy suppressed another giggle. "Liam isn't going to be too happy with your *mamm* when he finds out what *really* happened to that horse."

"Buttercup had a happy life, but she was very old. He knew that when he left. He knew she wouldn't last much longer, and he couldn't face it, just like he couldn't face the death of our *daed.*"

The conversation took a sudden serious turn, and Lucy didn't want to discuss it. Thinking of all the things Liam would have rushing to his memory of the past few years scared Lucy to her very soul. He would feel betrayed by her when he remembered they were no longer in love. Would he despise her for lying to him, or would he realize she'd done it to spare him additional grief?

Lucy walked toward the buggy, feeling like she was suffocating. She placed a hand to her heaving chest, willing herself to breathe in slowly so she wouldn't pass out. She knew her fragile heart couldn't take the pressure of being broken by Liam a second time, but she had to keep calm in front of Lydia. She was certain that when Liam remembered she'd rejected him all those years ago he would never let her back into his life. She didn't want to appear rude to Lydia, but she was in no shape emotionally to be discussing this any further.

"Wait for me, Lucy," Lydia called after her.

Lydia climbed into the buggy just in time before Lucy slapped the reins lightly against her mare. The horse trotted off down the long drive to the main road, while the two of them sat in silence.

Lydia put a hand on Lucy's arm. "I'm sorry. All this talk of Liam's memory must be upsetting you."

Lucy swallowed tears that felt as though they were choking her. "I'm afraid that if your *bruder* remembers we were apart all these years that he will leave me all over again. I don't know if I can handle the heartbreak a second time."

"I've seen the genuine love in his eyes when he looks at you. It's the same way he used to look at you when you were younger."

Lucy wiped away a tear. "That's because he thinks we are back there at that time in our lives. If he knew how things were between us now, he wouldn't look at me like that."

Lydia took the reins so Lucy could blow her nose. "Love like that doesn't go away so easily. You haven't stopped loving him after all these years. Perhaps it is the same for him."

Lucy tucked the handkerchief in her apron pocket. "I've been a fool to hope he'd come back to me after all this time."

"*Nee.* True love endures forever," Lydia said, trying to comfort her.

Lucy could not calm her galloping heart no matter how many slow, deep breaths she took in. Her nerves were twisted in knots, and her stomach roiled, making her wish she hadn't eaten.

"Maybe ours was not true love," Lucy cleared her throat to control the tears that made her voice squeaky, but it was no use. "That is why we are no longer together."

Lydia huffed. "You're no longer together because *mei bruder* has acted like a fool."

Lucy could see past the anger that twisted Lydia's face. She loved her *bruder,* but she was pledging loyalty to her friend. Lucy didn't want her to feel as though she should choose sides. Lydia was free to care about both of them, although Lucy had to admit it was nice to have a confidante.

"He did act very much like a fool," Lucy agreed. "But so did I. We were both too young to be making the kind of decisions he wanted us to make. Not to mention, he didn't give me more than a few minutes to think about it. Maybe if we had talked about it before he made up his mind, I could have helped him through whatever he was going through at the time."

Lydia shook her head. "*Nee,* he had to figure this out for himself. All you can do now is continue to love him and hope that when he remembers, he'll see that you stood by him all this time and appreciate you more for it."

"I pray that you are right, Lydia."

Lucy was tired of analyzing the whole thing. She knew the only way to really know if she was doing the right thing would be to jump in with both feet and hope for the best. She was in it for the long term, and she prayed Liam would see that when he regained his memory. If he didn't, then she had to prepare herself to walk away and move on with her life. She was certain she would never stop loving Liam, and prayed it was so for him too, but her heart would probably never let him go. She would remain devoted to him for as long as he would have her.

Chapter 29

Two days had passed, and Lucy had watched Lydia and Steve develop their friendship into something more, while she and Liam seemed to be at an impasse. All day at work, Lucy could hear Lydia and Steve talking and laughing while they worked on the quilt shop. They had made considerable progress, and the *menner* that worked for Liam had already installed the new ceiling. It was starting to look like a shop finally, and Lucy hoped Liam would be pleased with the work they had done in his absence. That is if he would ever remember his present life.

Lucy still couldn't be certain she wanted Liam to regain his memory, but it seemed things between them were a little strained. Maybe it was just her insecurities playing tricks on her, but she'd hoped things would progress between them a little faster. He was healing physically quite fast, but his spirit seemed a little sluggish, and that worried Lucy. She loved him more than anything, and wanted to be the one he would lean on, to be the one to make all of his pain go away, but she just didn't know him anymore.

When Lucy approached the clearing in the cornfield, Liam stood there waiting for her. His appearance startled her a little.

"You're up out of bed! Did Doctor Davis give you an exam today?"

Liam gently tugged on her hand, pulling her into the open yard. "He says I'm healing nicely, and it should only be a few more days before I can get back to work doing easy stuff—but no lifting for another week."

"*Das gut.* I hope your head is feeling better. How about your vision?"

She had to admit she was still a little nervous about having Liam see how she looked now. She felt so old suddenly, and very plain, and hoped he wouldn't dislike what he saw in her. She knew vanity was wrong, but she just couldn't push down the worries.

"Vision is improving, but I might still need a little help making my way around."

He patted her hand lovingly and tucked it into the crook of his elbow, escorting her instead of the other way around. She wondered if he was using his blurry vision as an excuse to be nearer to her, but she didn't care. She was happy for the closeness.

"Would you like to sit on the porch? I can go inside and bring out some tea or lemonade—whatever your *mamm* might have in the kitchen to drink."

He tugged her in the opposite direction. "I'm not thirsty; I'd rather take a walk down to the pond if that's alright with you. If I remember correctly, it's one of our favorite spots."

If he remembered correctly? What did he mean by that?

When they reached the edge of the pond, he didn't release her hand where it was tucked neatly in the crook of his arm. Lucy gazed upon the moonlit water as she took in the sounds of frogs singing to one another across the glass-like surface of the pond. Crickets chirped in the tall grasses to either side of the dock, and an occasional bird sent out a call to another, where an answer would come from a nearby tree. Lucy wasn't sure how long she could endure the distraction of nature that seemed to grow louder the more anxious she became. She had to break the silence, but what should she say?

"This pond hasn't changed one bit." He covered her hand with his free hand and gave it a squeeze.

Before she had a chance to think about it, he turned to her and pulled her close. "I've never stopped loving you, Lucy. You are the love of my life."

Lucy felt tormented. She wanted to lean into the strong plane of his chest and lose herself in the folds of his arms. Her conscience would not allow her to lie to him; she was compelled to tell him the truth no matter how much it hurt them both.

"You're not mine anymore…"

Liam interrupted her as his lips met hers. His soft mouth swept over hers making her hunger for more. She couldn't break from him even if she wanted to. Her will to do what was right became clouded in the delight of his lips against hers, making it impossible for her to think clearly. The sounds of the crickets and frogs became like delicate music in her ears, when only moments ago it had begun to annoy her. Suddenly everything felt right as a love so powerful surged through her, a love unbreakable by time or distance. Nothing would ever be the same for her again.

Liam couldn't resist Lucy's magnetic force pulling him further into the kiss. She smelled like baking spices and sugar, something he would cherish forever. He saw his future in the blue of her eyes, a future he could not bear without her tucked neatly at his side.

His mouth trailed to her cheek and toward her temple where he whispered his unwavering love for her. She would be his, and his world would be right again no matter what it took to make it so.

"I have never stopped loving you, and I want to spend the rest of my life proving it to you."

Regret would not overtake him for time lost between them, for he intended to make up for every day they'd lost over the past seven years.

She pulled away gently. "You remember, don't you?"

Liam sank to one knee in front of her, trying not to wince from the pain in his ribs. He swept his hand in hers and pulled it to his lips, allowing it to linger there for just enough time for her to catch her breath.

"I remember nearly all of it. There are still a few things that are a little fuzzy, but I remember how much I hurt you when I left here seven years ago, and I promise you I never intend to hurt you again. Please, Lucy, marry me so I can spend the rest of my days proving to you just how much I love you."

Tears constricted Lucy's throat. Was this really happening to her? Was this handsome *mann* she had loved since they were mere children really kneeling before her asking for her hand in marriage? She could see the sincerity in his eyes that pooled with the moisture of his emotion.

"*Jah,* I mean yes! I will marry you."

Liam stood faster than he should have and scooped Lucy into his arms, ignoring the pain in his ribs. His lips met hers again, and she leaned into the kiss, deepening it with all the love she felt for him.

With those three simple words, Liam had brought years of worry and angst to an end for Lucy. Her wait was finally over, and her future was about to begin with the *mann* she'd loved since they were both young. Her future was finally secure, and she would never again have to wonder if he still loved her or what could have been between them, because he was very much in love with her, and they were going to spend the rest of their lives together.

Chapter 30

Liam had no idea how he would break the news to his mother that he'd regained his memory. She'd gone to such great lengths to shelter him from the news of his father's death, and that of his favorite horse, that he didn't have the heart to hurt her again.

But tell her he must.

He'd enjoyed the last week with her and Lydia, and didn't want to break the bond they'd revisited. His love for them was steadfast, and they needed to know he regretted the decisions he'd made as a foolish youth. He intended to make up for lost time with his family as well as Lucy, but he wasn't certain how to approach the subject. He'd always jumped in feet first, but he was an adult now, and needed to control his impulsive nature to spare his mother and sister from further pain.

Liam stood in the doorway of the sitting room admiring his *mamm's* devotion to her quilting stiches. She had always sewn the most beautiful quilts, and the proof of that was spread among most every *haus* in the community. She was always making a quilt for a birth or a special occasion of some sort, and her unyielding allegiance to the recipient of the gift was a trait he admired most in her.

Emotions welled up in him as he watched his *mamm* from the doorway. How could he strip the smile from her face, when it had only just appeared when she'd brought him home?

Liam cleared his throat as he approached, hoping it would encourage her to acknowledge him before he lost his nerve. He crossed the room when she looked up from her sewing, and sank down in the chair opposite her.

"Steve tells me the quilt shop will be ready for you to go back to at the end of the week."

Nellie set her work aside, her face turned ashen. "You remember everything now don't you?"

Liam wanted to sit at her feet the way he used to when he was a young boy, but he had to be the man he'd grown into and show her he could take responsibility for his actions.

"I remember how much I hurt you and Lydia, and I'm sorry. I acted like a selfish child and I never meant to hurt you. I felt so much shame over *daed's* accident that I didn't think you wanted me around. If I'd gone with him that day, I might have been able to spare this family the pain of losing him. I might have been able to save his life, but I let him go alone because I'd stayed up too late with Lucy the night before and fell asleep in the loft. When he found me, I protested the trip and he allowed me to stay behind. I should have been there with him."

Tears fell from Nellie's eyes, and her expression turned soft. Her heart filled with remorse.

"If you had been there, I would be mourning the loss of my son too."

Liam stood up and ran his hand through his short hair, another reminder of his rebellion. "Isn't that what I've forced upon you all these years? My leaving had to have been just as painful as *Daed's* death for you, especially since I left of my own free will. *Daed* didn't choose to leave you, but I did."

Nellie reached out a comforting hand and placed it on Liam's arm. "If I hadn't been so consumed with my emotions at that time, neither of my *kinner* would have suffered. I couldn't be a parent to either of you then. If I had tried to talk to the two of you instead of letting you fend for yourselves, you might not have left. It's partly my fault that you felt you had no other choice than to leave. I've had to come to terms with that recently, and take a bended knee for abandoning you as your *mamm* during our mourning period."

She stood up and crossed to the window, looking out at the Graber's cornfield that was nearly ready to be harvested. "I let go of my faith during that time. Instead of leaning on *Gott,* I tried to come to terms with the loss on my own. I questioned *Gott's* decision to take your *daed* from us. I was angry and so filled with sorrow that I neglected to see that my own *kinner* suffered the same loss."

Liam stood behind her and placed a hand on her shoulder. "Please forgive me for leaving you when you needed me to step in and take *daed's* place at the head of this *familye*. I should have been brave instead of a coward. I should have stayed and taken care of his *familye* the way he raised me. I let you both down and betrayed *daed's* memory."

"I forgive you for leaving us," Lydia said from the doorway.

Chapter 31

Liam couldn't believe the transformation as he looked at the finished quilt shop. They had moved the last of his *mamm's* things into the building and she would be ready for the grand opening in the morning. He relished the excitement in her as she bustled about the shop straightening and rearranging everything until she was satisfied with its position in her shop.

Her shop.

The Quilter's Square quilt shop had become a reality for his *mamm*, right down to the old sign that she'd insisted on repainting herself. He'd never taken more pride in his work than he had in finishing the shop for his *mamm*. She deserved to have something she enjoyed after all the heartache she'd endured over the years. It was a blessing that had come from the pain of losing her husband.

Liam's crew packed up their tools and loaded up the trucks while he took one final look around. Steve walked out with Liam's *schweschder* giggling beside him. They'd been officially courting for a few weeks, and Liam couldn't be happier for them.

Liam was to meet Lucy next door at the bakery in a few minutes when she closed up her shop, but part of him couldn't pull himself from this moment. This quilt shop had brought him back to his *familye,* and to the woman he'd loved since they were children. But it was *Gott* who deserved the glory for healing their hearts and renewing their love.

Liam stepped over to the display of quilts his *mamm* had fashioned in the front window to draw in customers. Everything looked so professional and pristine; his *mamm* was going to be a huge success with her quilting. Her success as a person far outweighed anything she would achieve among the *Englisch.*

Liam sensed his *mamm's* presence behind him. He turned in time to catch the smile that spread wide across her face.

"*Danki* for this, Liam. Your *daed* would be so proud of the *mann* you turned out to be."

Liam tipped his head down. "But I'm nothing like him."

Merriment permeated Nellie's expression as she looked upon her son with adoration. "You don't need to be a farmer and plow fields to be like your *daed.*"

She placed a hand over his chest. "It's what's in your heart that makes you alike. He was a *mann* of honor, and you have followed in his legacy."

The warmth of her love penetrated his heart. He had found his way back to the life he'd spent so much time running from. Now, it seemed, he couldn't get enough of it.

&OCB

Lucy put the last of the pastries into a box to take back to the Yoder farm. She'd been spending every evening meal with Liam's *familye* that would soon be hers too. Afterward, Liam would take her for a buggy ride. They had spent many evenings discussing whether or not they would take the classes for the baptism into the church, but neither of them had made up their minds. Lucy had recently told Liam that he couldn't have one foot in both the Amish community and the *Englisch* ways, but she had begun to rethink that statement where it pertained to their future together.

Lucy had to admit that she liked the new Liam—the *Englischer.* She enjoyed taking rides in his truck just as much as she relished the buggy rides they took. Nellie hadn't pushed them into making a decision, and even the Bishop hadn't summoned them for a meeting, though they suspected it was imminent.

If it was left to her decision, they would remain in the community but separate themselves and live more as *Englischers* than Amish, but if she intended to marry Liam, he would have the final say, and she would accept it. She had no desire to wear trousers or learn to drive, but there was something intriguing about watching the *mann* she loved working at his own business, a business built on *Englisch* principles.

Liam's decision to leave the community had given Lucy the courage to openly express her desire to explore the possibility of joining the *Englisch*. She had always been too frightened to consider leaving the community, but with Liam by her side, she felt free to draw from his strength. His love and devotion to her was all she needed, the rest would take care of itself.

Chapter 32

Christmas day, Goshen, Indiana

Lucy sat in the rocking chair of her newly-built home and stared out the window at her husband as he shoveled the porch in preparation for their *familye* to visit. She sipped hot tea and huddled under the wedding ring patterned quilt Liam's *mamm* had so lovingly made for them.

Nearly weightless snowflakes drifted lazily about, while the sun fought to peak through the gray sky. It was still hard for Lucy to believe she and Liam had been married for nearly two full months. Since their engagement, they'd been in a whirlwind of preparations, between the baptismal classes and the baptism, and finally, their wedding.

Lucy looked around the room admiring her husband's handiwork. Their *haus* was the first that Liam's company had built from start to finish, and Lucy could not be more in awe of his talents as a contractor. She felt overwhelmingly grateful that the community, including her *daed* and *bruder,* had all joined together to help get it built so quickly.

Content with their decision to remain in the community, Lucy was happy especially now that they'd just received the news that she was expecting their first *boppli.* She had never imagined her life could be so full of blessings, when only a few short months ago she'd felt so hopeless. Lucy whispered a prayer of thanks, feeling overjoyed by all that she and Liam had endured.

The front door swung open, snow swirling into the *haus,* as Liam stomped inside. He pulled off his gloves and blew warm breath on his cold hands.

"It smells like Christmas in here. Are you baking my favorite cookies?"

Lucy smiled as he moved over to the fireplace to warm himself. "It wouldn't be Christmas without them."

He shrugged out of his coat, pulling something wrapped in white tissue paper from his pocket. Liam knelt down in front of his wife and unwrapped the paper to reveal a sprig of mistletoe and dangled it above her head.

"It wouldn't be Christmas without a kiss from *mei fraa,* either."

Lucy threw her arms around Liam and pressed her lips to his. It was the happiest she'd ever been, and with the *boppli* on the way, things were only going to get better.

The End…

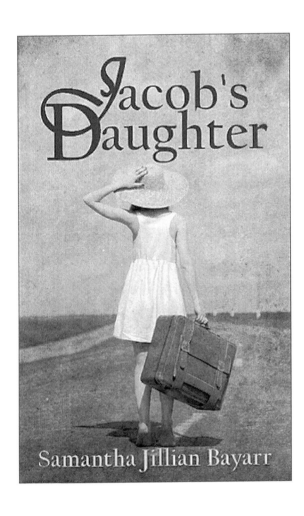

JACOB'S DAUGHTER

SNEAK PEEK PREVIEW

WRITTEN BY
Samantha Jillian Bayarr

CHAPTER 1

"I'm what?"

"You heard me, Abby. Now hurry up and put this dress over your head before we miss our bus."

Lizzie Barlow stood her ground. She could feel no sympathy for her daughter at the moment. They had to get on that bus to Indiana, and there was no time for the temper-tantrums of a ten-year-old to complicate their already life-threatening situation.

"I'm not Amish! You take that back!"

Lizzie pursed her lips. "Actually, Abby, you *are* Amish because *I'm* Amish."

Abby placed her hands on her hips in defiance.

"I'm not Amish! Why do I have to dress like them?"

Lizzie shushed her daughter, who was practically screaming.

She stamped her feet. "I want to go home right now!"

Lizzie firmly grasped her daughter by her arms and forced her to look at her. "We don't live there anymore. We have to go to Indiana. We'll make a new life there, and you'll love it so much you'll never want to leave."

Tears pooled in Abby's eyes. "If it's so great in Indiana, then why did you leave?"

The question pricked Lizzie's heart, and she was growing impatient with her daughter.

"It's complicated, Abby."

"Is it because of my father?"

Tears streamed down her cheeks, and Lizzie bit her lower lip to keep from giving in to her child's whims.

"We are *not* having this conversation right now. We're running out of time. Get dressed and we can talk once we arrive safely in Indiana."

"Why do we have to wear these awful clothes, Mom?"

Lizzie looked in the faded mirror in the bathroom of the bus depot, trying to wipe the remaining makeup from her face. "They aren't awful. And we're wearing them so Eddie's friends won't notice us if they should come looking."

"But I wanna wear my Hello Kitty shirt!"

Lizzie sighed. "Please don't make this harder than it already is, Abby. Slip this dress over your head, and hurry before we miss the bus."

She'd begun making the Amish dresses secretly, being careful to hide them from Eddie, Abby's drug-addicted father, so they would have them for their escape. Finding out he was Abby's father only three months ago, he'd threatened Lizzie that he'd kill her and take Abby if she wouldn't give him large sums of money to pay off his debt and support his drug habit. Lizzie didn't intend to stick around long enough to find out how much worse the situation with him would get. For weeks, she'd planned her escape from Eddie's threats, until the day he was found dead from a drug-induced, car accident that totaled Lizzie's car.

Dating him only two short weeks when she was still only seventeen, Lizzie tried to convince herself he was "the one" when they'd met, but she knew deep down she needed to end it with him so they could keep the passion between them respectable because he was a pushy *Englischer*. Sadly, she knew she could never really love him as much as a person ought to in order to take their relationship to the next level. She'd given her heart to only one man in her life, and she knew she could never feel that way for another. But when Eddie took advantage of her, she was left pregnant and ran from him.

Despite changing her name, Eddie still managed to locate her. And that's when the threats began. He demanded money from her to keep quiet about being Abby's father, and started threatening her when she wouldn't give him any more. Trying to spare her daughter from knowing the ugly truth of how she came into the world, she gave in to Eddie's threats until she just couldn't take it anymore.

Lizzie didn't make much money as a pharmacy technician, and when Eddie learned of her employment after coming into the pharmacy to try to redeem an illegal prescription for pain meds, he tried to force her to steal prescription medications for him. Out of fear of what he might do, she'd promised him she would do it, even though she had never stolen anything in her life, and she wasn't about to start. She'd managed to keep him at bay for a couple of days by telling him she hadn't found a way around the cameras in the pharmacy, but when he began showing up at her job, threatening her and her fellow employees, Lizzie was fired. It was too late for her to wish she'd moved farther away from him than the next small town over.

That same day, Eddie stormed out of the pharmacy in a rage of anger, and then totaled her car that he'd been *borrowing* by running it into the side of a tree, ending his battle with drugs—and his life.

Lizzie hadn't even cried. It wasn't that she was heartless, or didn't care that he'd died—she'd done her crying ten years earlier when she decided to leave him after he violated her. In truth, it was over between them the day that he drugged her and stole her innocence.

Still, she could feel little more than relief that her nightmare with him would be put to rest along with his remains. Though Eddie's pain and suffering was ended, her anger over the mountain of debt she was left with due to his reckless behavior had all but destroyed her. Not to mention the threats from the men who wanted her only child in exchange for a debt she didn't owe.

Because she'd let her car insurance policy lapse to give money to Eddie, she was stuck with a car that was no longer drivable, but was still responsible for the payment. And when those thugs started threatening her over the money that Eddie had borrowed from them and for drugs he had never paid for, Lizzie knew it was time to leave this life of debt and pain behind—for Abby's sake—and for her own peace of mind. Her mistakes in judgment had caused her ten-year-old daughter more harm than she was capable of understanding at her young age, and Lizzie knew what she had to do; it was time for her to face the sins of her past, and suffer the consequences to spare Abby from being caught in the middle of her poor choices any longer.

Losing her job, her car, and the threats from the drug-dealers all in a week's time was too much for Lizzie to handle. She'd seen the men before, and even witnessed them roughing Eddie up one night outside of her small, rented house. That's when she heard him promise them Lizzie could get them drugs. And that's when she decided the only way to get away from the thugs that were threatening her was to continue her original plan and find a place to hide from Eddie's mistakes; a place no one would ever think to look for her.

The Amish community.

No one knew of Lizzie's past—not even her own daughter. Given the nature of the events that prompted her to flee from the only way of life she'd ever known, she determined over the years to keep her past hidden, and had even practiced continuously to lose her German accent, and pattern her life after the *Englisch*. She determined, however, to maintain the teachings of her upbringing–even if only in secret. So far, she'd managed to keep her past hidden all these years, and now she was about to walk right back into it with Abby in tow.

Lizzie pulled the plain shoes and stockings from the backpack where she'd kept them hidden for weeks, and handed a pair to her daughter. "Put these on. We have to hurry and pin your hair up in the back."

Abby was busy texting her friends, probably telling them how unfair her only parent was being at the moment, and Lizzie knew it was going to be an even bigger argument when she broke the news to her daughter that the phone would soon be turned off due to non-payment. She reminded herself that it was for the best, since she wouldn't take any chances that Eddie's drug-dealing friends could use the device to track them down. She would have to wait for a while to get a new phone; necessities were the only thing they had money for until Lizzie could find a new job.

She would also worry about getting a cheap car once they got to Indiana; she would use a portion of the money she'd gotten from selling all of their things on Craig's List. She would need a car to look for work so she could find a small house to rent for her and Abby to start over.

Lizzie pulled her hair up and twisted it at the base of her neck, pinning it in place. She placed a prayer *kapp* over her head and handed the other one to Abby.

"Where did you get these weird hats?"

"They're called *prayer kapps*, and I made them."

"How do you know how to make this stuff?"

"YouTube has a video for everything; you know that." She wasn't exactly lying. YouTube did have a how-to video for practically everything, but Lizzie already knew how to make the *prayer kapps*, but she wasn't ready to tell Abby the entire story of her past just yet. She would save it for when they were far enough away from Ohio that she could relax enough to tell her everything.

When they were completely dressed in their disguises, Lizzie took one last look in the mirror. She never intended to wear Plain clothing again—let alone to walk back into Amish territory, but it was out of necessity that she would brave this move.

Without makeup, Lizzie thought she looked well beyond the twenty-eight years that she was, and getting pregnant at seventeen had not helped matters. It was more likely that all the hardship of the past years had aged her. Deep down, she knew some fresh air and a good dose of home-cooking was all it would take, and she'd be good as new.

As they exited the bus depot restroom, Lizzie looked over her shoulder to make sure no one had followed her and Abby. Just a few more minutes and they would be on the bus and on their way to Indiana where Eddie's *friends* would never suspect to look for them.

She *had* to go back home.

It was her only chance of escaping from her life with Eddie for good. Lizzie's own mother had died when she was Abby's age, and if her father had known about Abby, he would have shunned her. It was probably the best thing for her at the time to assume she'd been shunned, since it forced her to grow up and go to college. But even her education couldn't save her now from the damage Eddie had done.

They boarded the bus, but only when it pulled away from the depot, did Lizzie begin to relax a little. Their immediate future was unsure, but her destination for now, was the Miller Bed and Breakfast just off County Road 27, near the home where she grew up.

An Amish Christmas

Coming November, 2012

Coming in 2013

Amish Love Series

An Amish Harvest

An Amish Courtship

An Amish Widower

Amish Sisters

Please visit me on Facebook:

http://www.facebook.com/SamanthaBayarr

♥ Many blessings to you ♥